KU-063-308

LOUISE REDKNAPP

You've Got This

And Other Things I Wish I Had Known

PIATKUS

PIATKUS

First published in Great Britain in 2021 by Piatkus
This paperback edition published in Great Britain in 2022 by Piatkus

1 3 5 7 9 10 8 6 4 2

Copyright © Louise Redknapp 2021

The moral right of the author has been asserted.

All rights reserved.
No part of this publication may be reproduced, stored in a
retrieval system, or transmitted in any form or by any means, without
the prior permission in writing of the publisher, nor be otherwise circulated
in any form of binding or cover other than that in which it is published
and without a similar condition including this condition being
imposed on the subsequent purchaser.

A CIP catalogue record for this book
is available from the British Library.

ISBN: 978-0-34942-805-5

Typeset in Palatino by M Rules
Printed and bound in Great Britain by Clays Ltd, Elcograf S.p.A

Papers used by Piatkus are from well-managed forests
and other responsible sources.

MIX
Paper from
responsible sources
FSC® C104740

Piatkus
An imprint of
Little, Brown Book Group
Carmelite House
50 Victoria Embankment
London EC4Y 0DZ

An Hachette UK Company
www.hachette.co.uk

www.littlebrown.co.uk

CUMBRIA LIBRARIES

3800305108852 4

I'd like to dedicate this book to anyone who has ever struggled to see a way forward in life, and I want to let you know ... you've got this.

CONTENTS

INTRODUCTION

$\mathcal{H}$i there,

Thanks for picking up *You've Got This*!

They say that change is life's only constant. It can come in many forms, whether it's the end of a relationship, a new career, a loss or even some kind of opportunity. Even though allowing change into your life can be hard, it can often be for the best. Change allows us to grow and pursue our dreams.

For a long time, I ticked all the boxes of being the 'picture-perfect' wife. I smiled and said the right things at the right times, and tried very hard to maintain that image and make everyone else happy. The truth? For a lot of that time, I actually felt lonely, anxious and unimportant. Many of us believe what we read, and see what we want to see, but often we can't really know or understand someone else unless we're walking in their shoes.

I've been in the public eye since I was just fifteen. Throughout my career, I've always said a lot and been honest, while at the same time trying to reveal as little as possible about myself. No one beyond my close friends and family has ever really seen the real me. For my whole life, I've been described as 'nice'. There are a lot of words I would use to describe myself – passionate, kind and emotional are just a few of them – so I hope this book will show that 'nice' Lou is not the only side of me.

Writing this book has required me to talk openly and address head-on some things that I would rather not have thought about, even though I knew I needed to. And I hope reading it gives you the strength to do the same. I want to share with you some of the lessons that I have learned over the years; not just in my personal life, but in my professional life, too. Much of what I have gone through has been very bittersweet; often, I knew I needed to do certain things, even when they were tough and scary. There have been times when I thought I would never get through it all. This is a good opportunity for me to talk about what I have learned, from both the good times and the bad. Some of these lessons have been hard-won, but I'm finally in a happier place, and I feel more optimistic and stronger than ever. I don't want to hide any more. I want to celebrate all the unique sides of myself without apology, and I'm excited about the possibilities in my future.

I want to empower you to be fearless so that you can be excited about what your future holds, too. Most importantly, I want you to know that, whatever you are going through – whether you want to overcome heartbreak, kick-start your career, deal with criticism, tackle negative body image, or redefine another part of your life – if you are positive and passionate, you can do it. You will come out the other side feeling a lot stronger and more resilient than you previously thought. Anything is possible when you have the courage to trust yourself.

Let's do this!

Love Lou x

Chapter One

OWN YOUR FEAR

'Becoming fearless isn't the point. That's impossible. It's learning how to control your fear, and how to be free from it.'

Veronica Roth

'What are you going to sing for us today, Louise?' The panel of judges and teachers sat in front of me at a long wooden table and stared out expectantly. It was like a scene out of *Flashdance*.

'I'm going to sing "I Will Survive" by Gloria Gaynor,' I replied. Bubbles of excitement fizzed inside my stomach, drowning out the sharp prick of nerves. I was auditioning for a scholarship at the Italia Conti Academy of Theatre Arts.

There was an uncomfortable pause. Four sets of eyebrows raised slightly.

'Go ahead.'

I fumbled in my pocket. 'I have a tape. Is that OK?'

Someone nodded, and the pianist sitting in the corner turned away from me. I shuffled towards the cassette player, fumbling as I placed the tape into it and pressed play. The quality was very fuzzy, like a poor radio connection. I was using the backing track on the B-side, which I had recorded from the original. It was a long way from the polished performance that I imagine many of the other kids were going to present to the panel that day. I had no professional sheet music like the other girls and boys outside, who had been practising their melodic warm-ups before launching into songs from *Annie* and *The Sound of Music*.

I walked back into the centre of the room, my footsteps echoing across the parquet floor.

I took a deep breath and began to sing.

As I started to sing, my nerves fell away and my voice grew confident and bold. I had always been told that my voice was quite low and mature, and not what anyone expected from a skinny ten-year-old. I had grown up on a musical diet of the Motown greats, with Stevie Wonder, Marvin Gaye, Randy Crawford and Diana Ross firm favourites. Pop music wasn't on my radar; these were the songs I knew and loved. For me, music was all about driving bass lines, gospel-influenced harmonies, and bags of sass, guts and soul.

As the chorus kicked in, I launched into the dance moves I had practised in front of my bedroom mirror with my hairbrush as a microphone. Singing and dancing were always what made me happiest, and

I quickly forgot about where I was and the faces watching me.

x x x

I had discovered when I was very young that there was something about performing that made me come alive. Mrs Miller, the softly spoken and kind-faced headmistress at the small Catholic primary school I attended, St Thomas Moore's in Eltham, had suggested to my mum that I try out for an ILEA scholarship, which would allow me to attend a performing arts school. She could see that performing was what made me tick. Although I'd never done anything like it before, the audition sounded like a fantastic opportunity. Mrs Miller encouraged me to just go along for the experience, and Mum agreed.

I still remember the incredible kindness Mrs Miller showed me as a child; she really went out of her way to help me and took both Mum and me under her wing. And although I struggled through maths, English and other schoolwork, which affected my confidence, I lit up on stage. Mrs Miller saw that I became someone else when I was performing – a bolder and more confident version of myself. I have many fond memories of our school shows. One of my highlights was when I played the role of the Christmas Rainbow. I wore a white leotard covered with coloured streamers, which my mum had spent hours sewing on. I was always full of energy, which meant I was never calm enough to be Mary in the nativity. In fact, I sometimes wonder if the teachers were forced to write special parts for me – ones that involved spangly leotards and jazz hands. Not that I complained. I've always given my all to every perform-ance, so although the Christmas Rainbow was only a small part, I really belted out my lines.

Every year, I entered the singing, dancing and drama competitions at the Lewisham Dance Festival. Once, I even entered a TV competition for schools to write and perform a song on the day of Prince Andrew and Fergie's wedding. I composed a song with a boy in my class named Andrew – and we won. The whole class had to perform our song live on *Breakfast Time*. While the other kids sang with straight faces, looking as if they would rather be anywhere else but on TV, I was standing on the edge of the row, clicking my fingers and wiggling my shoulders, with my pink jazz shoes on, having the time of my life.

Despite all the encouragement I was given, I don't think anyone thought that I had a chance of being awarded the scholarship. There were around a hundred children outside the room that day, waiting for their chance to sing and impress the panel, and I knew there were auditions being held every day that week, but just four scholarship places were available: two for Conti's and two for ArtsEd.

'Just have a go, Lou, and see how you get on,' my mum had told me. 'You have nothing to lose.'

That morning, we had travelled to the Barbican from

our home in Lewisham. It was rare for us to travel into central London, and as we walked hand in hand along Goswell Road, I remember staring up at the high-rise concrete in wonder.

Mum dropped me off in the grand reception hall, where pictures of the famed and celebrated alumni hung from the walls. I felt the pins and needles of nerves, but these were extinguished by the anticipation and exhilaration of simply being there. I was totally fearless, and I felt no expectation or pressure to succeed. It was just one big adventure.

I was aware of the other kids around me, with their Head bags and professional dance shoes and kit. They had a quiet, shiny air of self-assured confidence about them, as if they were regulars on the audition circuit, but that still didn't faze me. I was convinced that the academic entrance exam had gone awfully. In the morning, there were dance classes – ballet, modern and tap – and I had done my best, performing everything that I had learned from my dance teachers, including Della Pointer, my strict elderly ballet teacher, who was renowned throughout Lewisham for her sharp words and impeccable standards. It had been all been a bit of a whirlwind of leg warmers and leotards.

The singing audition was the last part of the day.

As I finished the song, the teachers' faces were impassive, giving nothing away.

'Thank you,' one of them said, and I took that as my cue to leave.

I don't think they liked Gloria Gaynor, I mused as I closed the door behind me with a click. *Maybe they would've preferred 'A Spoonful of Sugar'?* I thought I'd blown it, but nonetheless a burning ambition started to grow. Whether I got in or not, I knew I wanted to be a performer.

Growing up, I was my mum's shadow. We led a pretty humble and simple life; it was an uncomplicated time. Mum had given birth to me on her own when she was just twenty-three, and after a year living in a mother-and-baby home, we had moved into a one-bedroom council flat in Lewisham, near her family and where she had grown up. Mum and I had a special bond: we were each other's whole world. Everything my mum did was about me and my happiness, and vice versa.

I never knew my father. He walked out of my life before I was born, and I've always been OK with that. Sometimes I think it's pretty strange that I could get on a train one day and not know that the person sitting next to me was my father, but I have no bad feelings towards him. There was always so much love in my life that I never felt like part of the jigsaw was missing. One of my aunts is still in touch with him, and I know he has his own family now. He once suggested to her that he would be open to meeting up and getting to know me, but I never wanted to create heartache for his family or my mum. Mum never asked him for anything, so now I feel that I owe it to her to never explore what could've been. Growing up, I never asked any questions, and now I've made peace with the fact that he is just part of my history.

My life was filled with laughter and love. I was very close to my nan and Grandad Malcolm, who owned an old-fashioned pub called the George Inn in Lewisham. Grandad Malcolm wasn't my mum's dad, but he'd been married to my nan since before I was born, so he was in my life from day one. He didn't have any children, so he always treated me like one of his own. I adored him and my nan, so I spent a lot of time at their pub during the holidays and on weekends. I played the Motown music that I loved on the jukebox in the corner of the pub, selecting my favourite tracks over and over again. Sometimes I would sit on the beer-stained bar and entertain the regular punters with a Motown or soul song through foggy clouds of cigarette smoke, and they always clapped and cheered at the end. After the lunchtime rush, the pub would shut for a couple of hours in the afternoon, and we would head upstairs and watch game shows like *Going for Gold* and *Bullseye*, with a packet of prawn cocktail crisps from the bar and a Kit Kat.

My other grandad, my mum's dad, whose name was Charlie, was a market trader at Lewisham market. Grandad Charlie was larger than life and such a gent; he was one of those people you could hear from a mile away cracking a joke as he sold his colourful medley of fruit and veg. He wore a crisp three-piece suit every day, with a waistcoat, cravat, hat and Crombie coat. He was the smartest man you could meet and such a character. He always had a fifty-pound note in his back pocket. He simply worked until he got what he needed through the strength of his personality and work ethic. Mum says that I was always his favourite; I never went without when Grandad Charlie was around, and he used to sneak me notes and coins from his money belt with a wink every time I saw him. Our family was one big gang. My mum was close to her sisters and brother, and at Christmas we would all spend time together, inviting Grandad Charlie so he was never left on his own. Even now, it's the same. When it's someone's birthday or we have something to celebrate, family is always at the heart of it, and everyone piles around the table.

Mum worked hard to survive and get me everything that I needed – and I'll be forever in awe of her. Some days she worked on Grandad Charlie's stall; on others, she'd take on cleaning and ironing jobs to make sure she was earning enough to keep a roof over our heads. Often, she would pick me up after school and bring me along to the office she cleaned at night, and she'd give me a couple of small jobs to help out with. She was a grafter. When Mum was working on the stall, I would sit with my cousin among the cardboard boxes beneath the green tarpaulin-covered tables, listening to my Walkman or drawing.

As soon as I was old enough, I was at singing, dancing, or swimming lessons almost every night of the week after school. Mum was determined to give me a good start in life. She didn't want me to be watching TV and sitting around doing nothing in our flat. Even at age four, I would put on shows for Mum in our living room and sell her a twenty-five-pence ticket to watch. I would strip the furniture to make a stage, and God help anyone who tried to leave before the final curtain! Mum even arranged for me to have speech and elocution lessons with a drama teacher who lived nearby. She said that she wanted me to be able to hold my own in any room, anywhere in the world, and not be held back by where I was from. We joked that I was the poshest council flat child in the area. She opened up the world to me, and I will always be grateful to her for that.

On the evenings I didn't have any after-school classes and Mum wasn't working, we would go to the nearby park or Eltham Common, and she would do her knitting, her needles clicking together, while I played on the swings or the slide. Although we never spent much time in the flat, she would always urge us to get back home before it was dark outside. We lived on the thirteenth floor, and we never knew who we might meet in the lift, or in the dark and evil-smelling stairwells when the lift was out of order. I was pretty streetwise, having grown up in the area, but I also knew to always try to avoid trouble. On the whole, though, I loved Lewisham, as it was such a melting pot of cultures and people. For a long time, my best friend at school was a girl called My, who had come over to live in London from Vietnam with her family and spoke no English. Somehow, even though we could didn't speak the same language, we struck up this fantastic friendship. When Mum asked who I would like to come to a birthday tea in the flat when I turned six, My came, and we sat around the tiny table with my dolls and teddies. Sometimes, when you click with someone, it's an emotional connection – and the friendship is completely effortless.

When I was eight, we moved into our very own house on Birdbrook Road on the Brook Estate nearby. We loved that little house, and tried to work some magic on the place. The garden had been completely neglected and was overgrown with weeds, and the carpets and wallpaper inside were ugly and faded, but we loved it anyway, because it was ours.

Mum only ever went out once a week, on a Sunday night, and she started dating the man I call Dad, whose name is Tim Nurding. He was a builder. One night, shortly after they had met, she joked to me that, even if the relationship didn't work out, 'He might be able to help sort out the fireplace!' Despite her joke, we had become very self-sufficient, doing lots of DIY and moving furniture around when we felt like changing things – we even earned ourselves the nickname 'Lynne and Lou's removals' at one point. Even now, Mum and I make furniture and do lots of DIY and upcycling together. My mum and dad fell in love, and Dad quickly moved in with us. He was a massive Motown fan, too, and loved Stevie Wonder and Smokey Robinson, so they were always blasting from the stereo. The music used to drive Mum mad, and she would always be turning it down, but Dad or I would turn it up again as soon as her back was turned.

Tim was the first and only dad I have ever known. I remember him telling me one day that if I wanted to call him Dad, I would be welcome to, and it would make him really happy. A few days later, as I left the house to go to school, I shouted, 'See you later, Dad.' It was the most amazing feeling: I felt I could burst open with pride.

When Mum and Dad got married a year or so later, Dad legally adopted me. We went to court, where we all sat in front of the judge, and when they asked me if I was happy and wanted to be adopted, I gave them a resounding yes. By then, my little brother Joe had arrived, so we were a family of four. Mum and Dad's wedding was quite low-key, but lovely, and I walked behind my mum down the aisle. She wore a cool, calf-length vintage dress and I wore a Laura Ashley number in a similar style. My school choir sang in the church, St Mary's in Eltham, and it was just a perfect day. It made me so happy to see my mum looking so content. It had been just the two of us for such a long time, and as much as I had loved it when it was just Mum and me, now I had a dad and a baby brother, and it was so exciting to be part of a new, bigger family.

Sam arrived two and a half years after Joe, and all three of us have always been extremely close. When Joe was a baby, I was still quite young, so I didn't get too involved, but I was fourteen when Sam was born, and he always says it is like having a second mother.

When he was small and crying upstairs in his cot, my mum would tell me to leave him to see if he could settle himself and go off to sleep, but I always found it impossible. At even the smallest whimper, I would be up the stairs in a flash to pick him up, give him the biggest cuddle and gaze at his toothless grin. As my brothers got older, I would always look out for them. Sam is smarter and more put-together than all of us, but I am still really protective of him. Funnily enough, both the boys didn't even realise that we were only half-siblings until they were well into their teens.

Although I got on well with my dad, he could be pretty strict, and his relationship with Mum was volatile and difficult at times because of his unpredictable temper. It wasn't always easy, but he was a great dad to me. I think he gave me a lot of the fight and resilience that has got me to where I am now, and it's because of him that I was such a fearless child. Had I looked out of my bedroom window and spotted someone climbing over our gate, I would have called my dad before the police, because I've always known that he would protect me from anything.

We'd been living at Birdbrook Road for around two years by the time I auditioned for Conti's. I think my mum may have secretly hoped I wouldn't get in, as it would open up a whole new can of worms: how would she get me to school in central London every day, and how would she afford the expensive uniform and school trips? It's only now that I realise how hard it must've been for her to have to think about every single penny we spent.

I remember the day the letter arrived, because it was my eleventh birthday. Mum and I ripped it open. My heart was pounding, even though I fully expected it to be a polite rejection.

'We are pleased to inform you that we would like to award you an ILEA scholarship for Italia Conti Academy ... ' Mum read.

She didn't need to read much further before I was whooping with elation. I don't think I could've received a better present. And just as they always had in the past, Mum and Grandad Charlie made sure I wouldn't go without. Between them, they worked out how they would get me to school every day and pay for all the additional things that I needed.

I had no idea what stage school would be like. In my mind, I was picturing the scene from *Fame*, with everyone dancing on taxis in the street. Obviously, it wasn't like that – but I still adored everything about the school from the second I set foot there. I was eleven when I started, and it was the beginning of secondary school. All my friends in Eltham went on to the local comprehensive school, so I didn't know a soul at Conti's. I just got on with it.

One of my close friends tells me that I walked into Studio 41 on that first day, wearing a blazer that was massively too big for me (so it would last a few years) and, sounding super confident, said, 'Right, then: let's go to dance class!' It's funny, because confident is definitely not how I'd felt at the time. I quickly found a group of friends – Kéllé, Leticia, Sophie and Catherine – and we became pretty inseparable. My friend Charli joined us a bit later, but at the start, that was our little crew.

For my first few days travelling into Conti's, Mum came with me on the tube, but it meant four hours a day of to-ing and fro-ing for her, so a week later, she sent me off on my own. I would always get on the fourth carriage, and Mum would be waiting in exactly the right spot on the platform when the train arrived at Lewisham station.

I moved happily through the school days, with workouts first thing, followed by our dance and theatre classes. On some days, I couldn't believe that they were calling this 'school'. I loved it, and spent all my time focusing on my dance and drama lessons. Dance was such a big thing in our lives – we were always at it.

There was a studio on the same level as the canteen that was run by an amazing teacher, Chris Baldock, who taught street and jazz. (His sister, Wendy, eventually became one of Eternal's managers through the years.) We loved his class; it was an absolute favourite. We told him we'd been asked to cover up the glass door with paper because there were so many people coming in and out of the canteen. In reality, we just wanted to spend all afternoon in his classes, missing our 'proper' lessons, and we wanted to make sure no one spotted us. His class would last for at least three hours, and by 3 p.m. we'd have nailed the routine.

Our lessons for academic subjects were always in the afternoon. English and maths were tricky for me because I'm dyslexic. One of my least favourite things was sight-reading in our English class; I would always read a couple of paragraphs ahead, so that I was prepared and knew what I had to say when it was my turn to read. I had great relationships with my teachers, but I was hopeless at lessons. I still worked hard, though, both because of the work ethic that had always been instilled in me, and because I was determined to make the most out of the chance that I was being given.

People have this idea of stage schools as being hyper-competitive, full of kids pushing themselves to the front, but that really wasn't my experience at all. My friends and I just did our own thing and had a laugh. Nor was it the hotbed of privilege you might imagine. Like me, many of my friends were from 'normal' homes and their parents worked really hard to afford the fees.

When I was fifteen, we moved out to Surrey. Joe and Sam were getting older, and Mum and Dad wanted to be able to afford a bigger home. My dad ended up doing a lot of the work on the house himself. Soon after we moved, a letter arrived stating that because I was no longer living in London, I had lost my scholarship. I tried for another one, but it didn't work out. I was devastated. But as was so often the case in my childhood

and teenage years, I was shown real kindness and gen-
erosity. The school had invested a lot of time and energy
in me by this time, so they told me to keep coming to
class even though my fees had not been paid, saying
they would sort something out. In the end, the wife of a
local MP, who was very involved in a charity that helped
young people in the arts, arranged for half of my fees to
be paid, and my Grandad Charlie paid the other half. I
will be forever grateful to them for helping me continue
my journey at Conti's.

Sometimes there would be auditions for commercials,
or TV shows like *Grange Hill* and *Brookside*. One of the
first things we learned at school was that we wouldn't
get every job we went for, and that auditioning was
a process: it was about going along and having the
experience, in much the same way that Mrs Miller had
encouraged me to go for the ILEA scholarship. There
would be times where I would go to auditions with ten
other kids in my year, and no one would get the job –
and it never mattered. At that age, I was just willing to
try and embrace every opportunity that came my way.
Being able to train with so many talented friends was
an incredible experience. I did do the odd thing, like a
Kool-Aid commercial, a panto and the Children's Royal
Variety Performance. There were performances all the
time and open classes for people to come in and watch
us. I never got the lead parts, but I didn't feel envious
of the girls who did. I just hoped that if I kept working
hard, success would follow.

As I moved up through school, I wasn't sure what I was going to do when I left. I've always been a live-in-the-moment kind of a person, so I took every day as it came. A lot of the older kids went on to get jobs in the chorus of shows like *Cats* or *42nd Street*, and the school fostered such a sense of camaraderie that we were all really excited whenever anyone went for something and got it. It was a really supportive environment. I hoped that, when my time came, I'd follow in their footsteps and get a job in a chorus in a show on the West End or a small role in a touring production. Although I could never quite picture my future, it felt like I was on my way to good things.

Like any teenager, I spent a lot of time with my friends. We adored each other. I still love my friends now, but at school you are completely immersed in each other's lives, and you know each other inside out. Catherine lived on an estate in Pimlico, which was closest to the school and the main parade of shops there, so we would often hang out on street corners – not doing anything bad, just being teenagers. Leticia was always the naughty one with the boyfriends, but the rest of us never really attracted male attention. We had mates who were boys, and there were other local kids around who we might hope to bump into outside the sweet shop, but we were very innocent. My favourite thing from the off-licence was sucky sweets, a bag of crisps and a bar of chocolate. It's only now I'm in my forties that I'm being badly behaved!

On weekends, we would hang out or go shopping. We used to go to an indoor market which was by the Bluebird on the King's Road. I was one of those girls that saved every bit of my Christmas or birthday money for one thing that I would have my eye on for months. While my friends would buy whole outfits from Tammy Girl every week, I would save up my pennies for that one single thing. I remember one pair of John Paul Gaultier shoes that caught my eye. They were these flat trainers with an open back – pretty hideous, in retrospect – but I loved them, and when I could finally afford them, I was delighted. I'm still really into fashion, and I think it's my mum who got me into clothes. When I was younger, I used to love looking at what she wore when she went out, because she was always super-stylish. My favourite outfit of hers was a pair of cream-coloured, wide-legged suit trousers that reached right down to the ground, which she'd pair with a cream Jimmy Choo-style high heel, and a shirt and jacket. Looking at her, I'd glow with pride, because I always felt that she was the most fashionable woman ever. She was also the first person I knew to have a Club Sport tracksuit – they were massive in the 1980s. If my mum was wearing it, it was bound to become a big trend sooner or later.

From time to time, my friends and I used to go to clubs to dance, and it could be a real challenge getting past the doormen because I looked about twelve. Our outfits of choice would always be crop-tops and jeans, no high heels, so we never looked older than we were.

I wasn't interested in drinking – we were all dance students, and the thrill for us was hitting the dancefloor. One of our favourite haunts was a massive nightclub in Victoria called SW1. We always seemed to be able to get in, and I really fancied one of the bouncers who worked there. Obviously, I was a child, so the bouncer was not remotely interested in me, but whenever the song 'Finally' by CeCe Peniston came on, we would be straight up on the podium, trying to catch his eye. We were in our element.

One evening, I was out along Tottenham Court Road with Catherine, Kéllé and Leticia. It was shortly after my family had moved to Surrey, and I was staying over at Kéllé's that night. Kéllé and I had been firm friends since our first day at school – we just clicked. We were in a lot of the same dance classes because we were at similar levels, so we worked towards the same grades and exams together.

The four of us were on our way back to the tube, but as we walked past the Milk Bar, the bouncers shouted to us, 'You girls not coming in?' Even though we didn't go clubbing that often, on this particular night, it was all the encouragement we needed. Once inside, we pooled our money and found we had enough for two drinks between us. We hit the dancefloor. Pete Tong was DJing – this was before he was a massive name. I was always worried that my mum would kill me if she found out I had been in a bar – it was a running joke with my friends that Louise *Wood*er (my original surname) but her mum wouldn't let her – but I was still young and fearless, and we were really only there to dance and have a laugh with each other.

As we danced, a man came over. 'Can you sing as well as you dance?' he asked me.

'Yeah, I go to stage school. I love singing,' I said.

'I'm a manager, and I'm looking for young female singers. If you really can sing, then give me a call,' he said, giving me his card.

I tucked it into my pocket. 'Thanks, I will,' I replied.

His name was Denis Ingoldsby. He would become the manager of Eternal.

You've Got This . . .

Put your best foot forward – in your best shoes

Fear is an emotion that we all come up against, no matter where we are in our lives or careers. I wish I could bottle the child-like innocence and fearlessness I used to have when I was growing up. I had no fear of failure or of stepping out of my comfort zone, and I was always ready to take a chance, keeping an open mind about what might come my way. Nothing held me back; I just did my own thing. I don't think it ever crossed my mind what would happen if I made a mistake or if something didn't work out – and somehow, everything always turned out well. I just grabbed every opportunity that came my way. I was incredibly lucky that so much kindness was shown to me in my early life; by my family, by teachers and even by strangers, like Mrs Howe, the wife of the MP who organised for some of my school fees to be paid when I lost my scholarship. I think kids see the world through different eyes. They don't perceive limitation in the same way as adults. Rather than getting caught up in thinking about the 'What ifs?', they just move forwards with a sense of imagination, fun and openness to new opportunities. I wish we were more like this as adults.

Have you ever been so fearful about failing at something that you didn't even try it?

Many of us have experienced this at one time or another throughout our lives. Maybe you do a job you no longer enjoy, but just keep going with the flow because it seems easier and safer than trying something different? Or perhaps you're in a relationship that you feel is no longer working, but you're too nervous to do anything about it?

Fear controls so much of what we do, because we can't know for certain what the future has in store for us. If only we could accept that fact and let go of the fear we would be more open to opportunities and possibilities. Later in my life, I let the fear of failure cloud my decision-making. When I was pregnant with Charley, I made a new album, but I didn't release it. I was worried that it wouldn't chart, or that I might be dropped by my label, or I might become 'that artist' who failed. The more time that passed, the more and more convinced I became that it would never be a good idea to release it. While I know these feelings are normal, I still wish that I hadn't made that choice.

Owning your fear is where true confidence comes from

I think fear is probably one of the most powerful emotions, and everyone experiences it in some form. Sometimes it's about holding your head up high and doing the things that scare you most, even when you don't know if you will succeed. I know there are times in my life when fear has stopped me from being the best at something that I can be. Sometimes, I let people underestimate me, through fear of not being liked or of upsetting someone. I did a stint on the judging panel for *So You Think You Can Dance?* and I sometimes held back from saying how I really felt. I wish I had just been honest, rather than trying to play the 'nice card'. It meant people didn't really get to see the real me, or to understand that I can be a force to be reckoned with. If I had that time again, I would say what I really think. I did an interview once with a magazine and in the finished article, the journalist talked about how I instantly tried to make her feel comfortable, at ease and welcome. She suggested that I had this down to a fine art, and she is not wrong. I have never wanted anyone to judge me on anything, and as a result I tend to overcompensate, so I have lost a bit of myself and my ballsiness along the way. Now, though, I am learning to own my fear and take more chances, even if they scare me.

Always have a clear sense of purpose

I have learned that it is easier to make decisions that aren't based around fear when I know exactly why I am doing something. If I have a clear vision of what I am trying to achieve, I no longer make excuses; instead, I take ownership and action, however nervous or worried I feel. The fear of the unknown can feel enormous, so sometimes I try to map out all the things that could happen or go wrong, including all the worst-case scenarios. When I have looked at it in closer detail, it usually doesn't seem like such a big deal, and I've come to realise that there are actually very few things that you can't recover from. Often my worries are completely irrational, and talking them through with my friends or my mum can really help. Having supportive friends and family and a good group of people around you is so important.

Owning your fear doesn't have to mean stepping on other people's toes

So many women pit themselves against each other, but I don't understand this mindset. It's something I see a lot in my industry, and I can never believe the lengths that some people go to in order to try to further themselves and hold others back. We all feel self-doubt, but by owning our fears, we have the ability to push through these feelings. Your success does not depend on the failure or success of others, and someone else's success never detracts from your own. We all need to carve out our own space and be happy there. I love watching women in the public eye who are authentic and honest, who don't care what people think – I admire that.

You have to trust yourself and understand that true fulfilment will often lie outside your comfort zone

Feeling fear but making small leaps of faith anyway is often the path to growth. I'm starting to understand that my successes have come from seizing the opportunities that came my way, rather than playing it safe or saying no. For a time, fear of failure, fear of change and fear of how I would be perceived stopped me from taking opportunities, but now I just face that fear. I feel like I got to a point where I had almost lost everything, so I had to go out on a limb and write music from the heart, regardless of what people might say about it. I've also learned that sometimes we worry about looking like an idiot in front of other people, but actually, they really don't care that much. Mostly, other people are too worried about their own fears and failures to pay much attention to yours. This was such a hard thing to learn, but I'm done with being scared. Don't get me wrong, the fear still creeps in sometimes – I just don't allow it to hold me back any more.

I love this quote by the legendary motivational speaker, Les Brown: 'The richest place on earth is not Dubai, it's not Beverly Hills or the Hamptons, it's the graveyard. The graveyard is the richest place on earth, because it is here that you will find all the hopes and dreams that were never fulfilled, the books that were never written, the songs that were never sung, the inventions that were never shared, the cures that were never discovered, all because someone was too afraid to take that first step, keep with the problem, or determined to carry out their dream.' Amen to that.

Chapter Two

YOU ARE ALWAYS
GOOD ENOUGH

'There comes a point when you have to realise
you'll never be good enough for some people.
The question is, is that your problem or theirs?'

Anonymous

Sitting on the enormous bed in my room at the
Mondrian Hotel, I could see the lights of Los
Angeles scattered below me. It was four o'clock in the
morning. On the TV in front of me, reruns of trashy
American sitcoms and soaps played out, and on the
bedside table sat the half-eaten bowl of Frosties that I'd
picked up from the local garage hours earlier. At about
midnight, I had tried to get to sleep, and had spent an
hour or two tossing and turning before giving up. My
mind was racing and my stomach churned. I couldn't
stop wondering what was going on at home and when
I would see my mum again. Strange thoughts kept

crossing my mind, and all I could think about was how much I missed my family, and how hollowed out and anxious I felt. I wondered whether there was a way that I could get home without being sacked. What if I broke my leg? Maybe there was some illness that could see me sent home for a few weeks, so no one would be too annoyed with me? I hadn't eaten a proper meal for days, and I felt like I was living off my nerves.

It was March 1994 and, at the time, the Mondrian was one of the best hotels in West Hollywood. Despite the luxury of my surroundings, I had never felt more lonely or homesick. We had just flown here straight from Asia, where we'd been promoting our album *Always & Forever*. Now we were recording new material. Easther sometimes liked to record her vocals late at night, and I always enjoyed those late nights in the studio, with the production team and engineers all having a laugh until three or four in the morning. Sometimes, though, we would finish at six or seven in the evening, and then the rest of the night was ours. This had been one of those occasions, and by the early hours of the morning, I felt like I had been on my own for days rather than hours. This was before everyone had mobile phones and internet access, so I felt completely cut off from my family and the rest of the world. The smallest things, like hearing the *EastEnders* theme tune, could remind me of home, and brought with them intense waves of homesickness and feelings of sadness, almost like grief. Those feelings sat so deep inside me and weighed me down, like a rock. I just didn't feel like me any more. It was strange feeling like this, because at the same time, I was so happy to be part of the band – and being in LA was like a dream come true.

We had been away from home for around nine weeks by that point, touring around Asia. Earlier that day, we had been told by our manager that we were going to fly to New York to record *The Tonight Show* and *The Jay Leno Show*, because it looked like the album was set to chart in the States. When he told us, I felt my heart sink to my shoes. It meant that it would be weeks before I could go home again, and I felt so sick. I missed that feeling of security that came from being at home and having people around who just got me. At times, with the other girls, I felt like I was stepping on eggshells in case I did or said the wrong thing. Small things, like journalists asking me questions directly in interviews, or me being moved towards the middle in photoshoots, could cause a frosty atmosphere. And I didn't want to be the cause of any negativity – we were all so young and trying our best.

I really tried to enjoy the experience, but I constantly felt like the dispensable one in the group. Some days, I also wondered whether the other girls would be happier if I wasn't around. But then I also felt guilty. What young girl of my age, given the life I was now leading, would be having thoughts like this? What was wrong with me? I knew how lucky I was and I didn't take it for granted, but I didn't want to admit to anyone, even myself, that I was miserable. It felt wrong to even think it. Apart from my mum, no one knew how I was feeling, and even then I think I probably hid the true extent of it from her.

By this point, the band weren't spending much time together. We all got on well, but even though the music worked and our voices gelled, I didn't always feel like we were that close on a personal level. I would've been happy to have a hot chocolate in someone else's room if it meant having some company for an hour or two, but it wasn't really like that. I don't think anyone was to blame: that was just our dynamic. When we imagine what we want from life, we often picture a sort of fairy-tale version of reality, but real life isn't like that. On paper, being in the band was everything I'd ever dreamed of, but I missed my family so much that these intense feelings of loneliness seemed to overwhelm everything else.

I always put on a brave face for work, but my lack of control over my own life was starting to manifest itself in other ways. There were times I felt the need to switch the light on and off ten times, or brush my teeth a certain number of times before I felt OK. I told myself that if I did this, I would have a better day the next day, or it'd ease my anxiety. I knew it was irrational, but I just couldn't stop. Everything felt so out of my control. I have struggled with this type of obsessive behaviour for over twenty years to lesser or greater degrees, and it's only now that I have really curbed it. But at the time, it felt like the only way I could exert some power over my decisions.

I was also losing weight. At around that time, I was barely seven stone. I didn't consciously avoid food or obsess over calories, but I was working hard and sometimes forgot about meals. I've never been a comfort-eater – I'm the total opposite. Whenever I'm anxious, I can't stomach anything. So when I headed back to my suite after a day in the studio, rather than order something like a burger and chips from the room service menu, it seemed easier to have a bowl of cereal. It was really the only thing that I could stomach, and I felt like I was running on adrenaline.

Eventually, after watching hours of TV, I dropped off to sleep and was woken by my alarm just a short time later. I had just got dressed and was ready to get on with the day when my management knocked on the door. I could tell there had been a shift.

'We need to send you home,' Denis told me. 'We think you could do with some time with your family for a few days.'

'But what about *The Tonight Show*? And *Jay Leno*?'

He shrugged. 'Don't worry about that now. There'll be other opportunities.'

I felt such a strong rush of relief that I thought I might cry. I couldn't apologise for the missed chances or even disagree with the plan. I just wanted to go home.

My return had already been mapped out by my management. There was a comfortable car to the airport, a club-class flight home, and another car back to my house. I was on autopilot.

When I stepped through the front door, wearing a tiny skirt and a top that was hanging off me, my mum looked me up and down and burst into tears. 'Lou, what's wrong with you? You look so unwell,' she said, wrapping me in a huge hug.

'I'm fine. It's all fine,' I told her. 'I'm loving it, but I just feel a bit lost. I need some time out.'

Around a week later, I was back in the studio with the girls again. I could feel they were frustrated that our US plans had been curtailed, and I couldn't blame them, but just a few days back in the comfort of my family had been enough to make me feel a bit more like myself again.

A lot of people don't want to ask for help; they don't want to seem weak or like they cannot cope. But being able to say that you need some time out when you're struggling is much braver – and healthier – than trying to keep on going when you are feeling low. On this occasion, I was lucky enough that somebody else noticed I was struggling and stepped in to make sure I got that time out. If you have ever hit a stumbling block in life, don't worry. Just take a moment, breathe and remember to look after yourself.

x x x

Looking back, Eternal's rise to fame is a bit of a blur.

After Denis handed me his card in the Milk Bar, Kéllé's dad picked us up from the bar and I stayed the night with her as we'd planned before going home the next day. I couldn't wait to tell my mum and dad when I got in.

The moment I burst through the door, I told them. 'Mum, Dad, you'll never believe what's happened. A manager gave me his card and asked me to call him!'

'What? Don't be ridiculous, Lou. He could be anyone,' Dad said.

'You can't go accepting cards from strange men,' Mum chimed in.

'But, Mum, this could be my big chance. Please! I've got to give it a go. You know you can trust me.'

'You're only fifteen years old. That card belongs in the bin,' Dad said. 'And don't even think about fishing it out.'

Fortunately, I was determined to make that phone call – and I'd already made a copy of the number on the back of my bus pass, anticipating my parents' resistance. A few months later, when I was almost sixteen, I finally plucked up the courage to call the number from the payphone at school, with all my friends around me joking and giggling.

Denis was obviously genuine, but I think he was surprised when I told him that I was still only fifteen. He asked if he could talk to my parents and whether he could hear me sing. I imagine me telling him that I could sing because I went to stage school didn't mean that much to him; he needed to know whether I could actually hold a tune. We organised for him to come down to see me at home and meet my mum and dad, and he sat in our kitchen as I sang 'Signed, Sealed, Delivered, I'm Yours' by Stevie Wonder. Thankfully, he seemed impressed.

'Wow. That wasn't what I was expecting. I'd love to get her into the studio,' he said, talking to my mum.

Mum was nervous about me getting to and from the studio. My brothers were still very young, so she had her hands full with them and couldn't taxi me around. Denis promised her that he would look after me and organise cars to make sure I always got home safely at night.

It was agreed; I couldn't believe it. One day after school the following week, I headed to MCA Studios in Hammersmith for the first time. I was beside myself with excitement and anticipation. There were loads of famous people wandering around, but everyone was really friendly and unstarry. Boy George came over and said, 'Hi.' I just kept telling myself, 'Keep cool, Lou. Keep cool.'

Denis introduced me to sisters Easther and Vernie Bennett, and we started singing together. They were a few years older than me and seemed so self-assured, commanding and on the ball. I was instantly blown away by their vocals and was completely in awe of them; they sounded just like the artists that I had grown up listening to, and they sang effortlessly, but with so much passion, soul and power.

As well as MCA Studios, we used to go to Sarm Studios in Notting Hill. Back in those days, you could almost live your whole life there, without the need to go anywhere else. There were five or six separate studios, and it was almost like being at someone's enormous house. There was a catering service, so you could order what you wanted to eat from a menu and the food would be brought to you. There was a big lounge area with TVs and a pool table, so when you were not recording, you could relax and put your feet up. There were always other musicians and loads of engineers milling around. Later, when I was working with the music producer Johnny Douglas on my solo stuff, George Michael was recording his album at the same time, and we would cross over in the studio. He was one of the biggest superstars that I'd ever met, but he was also the kindest, friendliest man, and so down to earth. He always had time for everyone. He would come bounding in to the studio, with his dog – who would normally eat my dinner! – running after him. Years later, in 2006, when he threw a concert for NHS nurses at Camden Roundhouse, I bumped into him backstage. He gave me a huge hug and asked how I was and how my career was going. There are very few people in his league who would do that.

In the early days, Easther, Vernie and I did a lot of backing vocals and would stack up our harmonies, blending them together. When you love singing and you get to sing in a booth, it's such a buzz. One thing I'll always remember about those early days in the band was that Vernie would bring lemon meringue pie into the studio with her – it was her favourite. We would just nibble at it all evening long.

We were never told we were going to be a girl group, but Denis said he was looking for a fourth girl to sing with us, so I told them about my friend Kéllé, and she came to the studio with me after school one day to audition for him. Everything just clicked. We sang some backing vocals and started to experiment with other tracks, and, as time went on, it was clear that Denis had a bit of a future planned for the four of us. Around that time, I had just done my GCSEs and was still at school during the day on their three-year students' course. I would do my schoolwork, then hop in a cab over to the studio and be home by the evening. No one at school really knew about the band apart from my close friends. Kéllé continued with me at Conti's, and Easther and Vernie were also busy working and studying, so sometimes it was hard to find the time to rehearse together, but we made the effort.

It was clear from the beginning that we all loved the same kind of music, and that's what really helped us to gel; we all knew exactly where we wanted to sit musically. We were all massive fans of SWV and En Vogue. I think if I was put into a band that was all about bubblegum pop, I would've really struggled – and there were quite a few of those types of groups emerging at the time. But we all knew exactly where we wanted to go.

Eternal just seemed to happen. After hours of dance

and singing rehearsals, we went to see Stock Aitken Waterman, Island Records and EMI. After singing a cappella for EMI in the park close to their offices, we signed a five-album deal with them. I was really naïve and just did what I was told. I was so blown away to be in a band, I would've done it for free – or even paid them! I literally never thought of questioning the terms or asking someone else for advice about the contracts. I just felt so lucky – and I still had a fierce, youthful tenacity. It felt crazy that someone was paying me to do something I had always dreamed of. I couldn't tell you what I earned during that period of my life, but I remember that in the beginning, they gave us £100 a week for our expenses, for things like buying dinner if we were working late in the studio. I remember never wanting to spend it on food, so I'd make do with a bowl of cereal and save my money so I could buy myself some clothes or shoes at the end of the month.

We worked really hard from the start. We would travel around in this beat-up old van to do gigs in half-full dodgy nightclubs in the middle of nowhere. At that point, we were not the kind of band that had our own PA system, so when we turned up, it was always an issue to find four working mics – and, more often than not, they would all have cables. Our dance routines were a big part of our performance, so we would spend the whole show trying to not fall over each other's mic cables while we moved around the stage. Sometimes, there would only be three working mics, so it might be a toss-up between having a mic with a cable or a wireless one that was actually completely dead. We either looked ridiculous because we were trying to dance while skipping over cables, or ridiculous because we were singing into mics that didn't work. We used to laugh a lot about stuff like that.

Our debut single 'Stay' was released in September 1993. I remember being in the kitchen at home, getting myself some breakfast, and hearing it play on Kiss FM. I couldn't quite believe that I was singing on a track that was being played on the radio. It's unusual for a first song to be so popular, and things really blew up. It felt like a golden time for music back then. We did all our singing live, and I felt so privileged to perform alongside such talented singers. Soon, there was a professional sound system, and we were supporting Dina Carroll on tour and playing at Radio 1 Roadshows around the UK.

In November 1993, we released our album, *Always & Forever*, which charted at number two and quickly became the best-selling debut album in the UK, selling well over a million copies. Our second and third singles, 'Save Our Love', and, 'Just a Step from Heaven', were released shortly after and just flew. It was hard to really see how big the band was getting because we were working so hard all the time. It all happened so fast, and just felt like one big adventure.

By this point, we were stuck on a hamster wheel of recording and promo. Every day of every week was mapped out, months and months ahead. I lived by a schedule and the same driver – a lovely, gentle man called Bill – would pick me up every morning and take me wherever I needed to go. If we were in the studio, he would be there at the end of the day to drop me home. Our lives were not our own, but it didn't bother me. I didn't want to be at the pub with my friends or going to clubs – I had always wanted to make music, and now I was doing exactly that. It was only when we went off on tour to America that I think I fully realised that the group had made it. My school called me in for a meeting and suggested that it was time for me to leave. My work schedule had become so busy that they thought some-one else would benefit more from my place. I'd known this would happen sooner or later, but it was still hard, because I was so attached to Conti's. It had always felt like a second home to me, and getting in had been my first lucky break.

As *Always & Forever* began to chart around the world, we went on back-to-back promo tours in different coun-tries. We would head to each country a month before the single was released and stay to promote it until after the release, then move on to the next location. It was com-pletely surreal, but our song was hitting the top ten all over the place.

During the early days, we had a great time. Easther and I used to have loads of fun together. We shared a sim-ilar sense of humour and a real zest for life. She had this infectious, loud laugh, and she would clap her hands and stamp her feet as she cackled. I couldn't help laughing along with her. When we were recording in New York, there were late-night cinema viewings that would start at midnight, so when we finished in the studio, we would head out and watch movies. As we were often jet-lagged, I always struggled to sleep, so we were happy to stay up. We would head back to the hotel at about 3 a.m. We usually stayed at the Paramount, which, at the time, was known for employing male models to work in the restaurant. Easther and I never missed breakfast, no matter how late we'd been up the night before – it was the highlight of our day. Not only was the granola out of this world, but it was being dished up by an Armani model in a tight white T-shirt and a smart suit. It was the same with the doormen. The Paramount was our favourite New York hotel, and every trip to the restaurant involved at least an hour's prep and a hair wash, before we gawped at the male models as we ate.

Once, when we were recording in Los Angeles, Easther and I called the lift in the hotel where we were staying, only to find it occupied by Mark Wahlberg (aka Marky Mark), who was a massive star at the time. Easther and I were giggling like schoolgirls.

'Hey, girls, where are you from?' he asked us, leaning up against the mirror.

'We're from London. We're here working,' I replied, trying to look serious and sophisticated.

'Oh. Well, we're having a party tonight in Suite 204 if you want to come?' he asked, as the doors opened. He left, and Easther and I squealed loudly.

I don't think we ever made it to the party in his suite, but Easther and I shared a lot of hilarious moments like that. If things had carried on in that way, I reckon I could've ended up being the devil on Easther's shoulder, as I was often the one saying, 'Let's do it, let's go to the party.'

Eternal were a constant feature in *Smash Hits* and *Top of the Pops* magazines, and we started doing more and more interviews and performances. We even went on to win awards, like Best Newcomers at the 1993 *Smash Hits* Poll Winners party. We could tell we were becoming more successful, because people started spending serious money on us. I can see how easy it would be to become self-indulgent in that kind of situation, because there are people running around after you, tending to your every whim, but I never felt comfortable with that – I could always make my own cup of tea!

In what felt like not much time at all, we were no longer getting ready in a squashed dressing room on top of each other but would have individual suites at a hotel nearby and then cars to the studio when we were ready. The hair and make-up teams also started getting bigger and bigger, though I was always the last one to get in the chair. These days when it comes to make-up, I always say to just go with what you love and feel comfortable with. If that's a red lip and some fierce eyeliner, own it. My preferred go-to look is something fairly natural on the eyes and a nude lip, but for those shoots we were often heavily made-up. When it came to clothing, though, we did a lot of our own styling. When we were in America, we would buy loads of baseball tops and wear them with cycling shorts and Timberland boots. The only time we had stylists was when we were filming our music videos, as for those the way we looked was much more mapped out and controlled, but beyond that, we just wore what we loved. Once, when we were in New York, we all bought massive Stussy jackets and decided to wear those on stage. We were very much our own people and would just turn up at gigs wearing whatever we wanted.

A big team of people grew around us, including security, and we never really saw anyone outside our own bubble. We never really got hassled by men: most of them would politely ask for an autograph and then run off. Some fans somehow worked out where I lived and would sit on the wall outside the house, and my mum would come out and offer them cups of tea and a biscuit. It was a different kind of fame then. There was no social media and no one could really get close to us. Despite the band's fame, I never felt that well known because we didn't have that much contact with the outside world. The way we listen to music has changed now, too. People are much more into just the music rather than the artist these days. Back then, it was more about the whole package and true fandom, where fans would come to every gig, buy all the memorabilia and join fan clubs. As we performed at more gigs, we started to recognise the same faces in the first few rows of our concerts. I just loved singing live to the audience. I'd look down from the stage and they'd know every word – you could stop singing and they would take over. My eyes would well up; there's no feeling quite like it.

When I was living at home and commuting to the studio, I was coping OK, but as we started to travel more and spend more time away, I began to feel increasingly lonely and anxious. I'm sure this is something that a lot of people who have spent time away from home can relate to. There was also a rule that we weren't able to bring anyone with us when we went travelling or to gigs. I started to feel like we weren't supposed to be having fun away from work, so in my downtime I would go to the gym, or eat cereal on my own in my room. It was weird and pretty sad.

The trips away were always different, and I found some easier than others. One of my absolute favourites was when we went to Nashville, where we spent some time with the Winans family, who were famous for their gospel music. We were working with the producer BeBe Winans, but the whole Winans family is huge in the music industry. We went to church with them and hung out with Whitney Houston and Luther Vandross. The Winans were so kind, warm and open, and always made you feel included. They would take us out for dinner and we'd just talk about music and life.

There were plenty of other high points and pinch-yourself moments. We were asked to perform at the Sultan of Brunei's son's birthday celebrations, and we learned that he'd also invited Whitney. It was completely surreal. We were all delivered to our separate houses in this huge gated estate. Cars then picked us up to go to the main house, which was like a palace. It was a kind of wealth I have never seen before or since: I remember one of the Sultan's sons had every supercar going in yellow. Whitney stood and watched our show and told us she loved it. She was my idol and had always been one of those artists that made me want to be a star. There are talented people and there are superstars – and she was an absolute megastar. I have never seen a vocal perform-ance like hers. I don't even have the words to describe her natural ability; it was simply breath-taking, awe-inspiring. I remember the goosebumps on my arms, and that I almost held my breath as she belted out some of her most well-known songs.

My proudest career moment to date was performing at an anti-apartheid concert in South Africa. It was the first concert that black and white people were allowed to attend together after the end of apartheid. It felt incredible to be performing at an event marking such an important moment in history, and something we all believed in so strongly; it feels crazy to think that during my lifetime people were separated in this way because of their skin colour. We supported Sting that night, and a sea of people stretched out before us as far as the eye could see. I think there were over 150,000 people in the crowd, celebrating, dancing and singing. I could never hear much on stage when there were so many people watching: it just felt like a buzz of energy pulsating through the air. Whenever I think back on Eternal, I remember what we experienced together as four young girls. No one else has ever lived those moments in the way that we did – and that one was magic.

We always performed live in Eternal and it was when we were together on stage, under the lights, that I felt closest to the other girls. There was never any bad blood when we were performing. We had our ups and downs, but musically we always had a great connection. We protected each other and there were never any 'Pussycat Dolls' moments of trying to outdo each other vocally. Whatever went on behind the scenes, we had each other's backs. Our performances would feature lots of quite complicated, full-on dance routines, and when you're singing at the same time, it's very easy to lose your harmony. Vernie is just such an incredible vocalist and her mind was like a piano. She could pick up any note she needed to in an instant. If I ever lost my harmony, she would look at me, put me back on my note and then go back to hers in the blink of an eye – and no one else would even notice. Although I love performing, there were many, many times that I really struggled. I never walked off stage feeling that amazing high that everyone talks about. I always worried about how it looked and how we sounded. Even now, after being in the industry for so long, I never feel like I have smashed it as I walk off. I always look at my manager or my musical director and I ask them if it was OK and how did I do? They're always very honest, so if they say it was good, I feel immense relief.

For the first time in my life, I became insecure. I felt that I had to fight harder than anyone else in the group to have a soulful voice and to be respected. I'd never been able to shake off the feeling that I was there to make up the numbers. Even now, when people tell me they were fans, I find it hard to believe. Easther and Vernie always had the lead vocals and made a lot of the decisions. Because I felt so vulnerable and unsure of myself, I didn't feel like my input mattered. I had this sense of being somehow expendable, and I would never put myself forwards. In fact, I began to shrink inwards. Although Kéllé and I had been friends for a long time, working together meant our friendship changed, and while I withdrew from the group, she formed a tighter bond with Easther and Vernie. As hard as I was finding some of the stuff that went on, I can see now, looking back, that it must've been hard for them to cope with my unhappiness, too.

When I flew home from the Mondrian Hotel and that LA trip, we all just brushed our feelings under the carpet. Since then, I've learned the hard way that it's always better to just lay it out in the open. If you approach situations with a level head and you're honest about how you feel, you can almost always nip things in the bud. The worst approach is to keep things to yourself because you're worried you might rock the boat, as ultimately you end up hurting yourself, and you deprive the other person or people of the chance to understand you and where you're coming from. Things don't just go away if you ignore them, they tend to fester. So even if it feels uncomfortable in the moment, always be true to how you feel. Looking back on it all now, I wish I had said what was really on my mind, or that we'd had a conversation about the dynamic and how we could make it better. But that isn't what happened. Our management and the teams around us could see what was going on, but no one did or said anything. I just carried on and kept going, putting on a brave face every day and smiling through it.

My departure from the band was not premeditated, and I had never seriously thought about saying I was leaving. After all, I had signed a contract. But one day, I was in the studio and a few things had been said, and that was it. It was a culmination of so many things, and I was just so tired. I placed my headphones on the stand, went out and bought myself a bagel from the café next door, then phoned Denis and told him I was leaving. There was something about that day that made me realise that no amount of fame or money or love of singing and performing was worth being made to feel the way I did. I was so proud of everything we did and I was a team player, but I couldn't live like that any longer. I don't blame the girls. I blame myself, in a way, for not standing up for myself and speaking out when I felt I wasn't being treated properly. I wish I had told them how I felt, but I'd already lost my confidence by that point.

I'm not sure anyone around us was surprised that I had taken the decision. I felt so relieved when I made the call. I understood what I was walking away from, but by that point, I didn't care. And I found that, in that moment of walking away, part of the old, fearless Lou had come back to life.

The next day, a team of management and execs came over and sat around my kitchen table at home. They told me they had signed up Eternal to support Take That on their upcoming European tour, and they needed me to go and do it. I never wanted to ruin the chances of the group, and really wished them well, so I was happy to. We agreed that my mum or a friend could come with me so I would have someone to keep me company.

A few weeks later, I was called into a meeting with the CEO of EMI Records, Jean-Francois Cecillon. Known to everyone as JF, he was always friendly, despite being an incredibly senior figure. Something that has always stuck in my memory about him was that he did his food shopping in the food halls of Harvey Nichols, rather than Sainsbury's like the rest of us. I knew immediately that anyone who could do their food shopping with a trolley in Harvey Nichols must be doing something right!

Walking into that meeting, I had no idea what to expect. I felt really guilty and had this urge to say sorry. I knew they had invested time and money in me, and I was worried I was letting people down. By this time, I had sat in plenty of big meeting rooms with lots of people, but I was still terrified. EMI had the power to make me stay and fulfil my contract. I was renting a nice flat at the time, and had enough money to live on, but there was no way that I could have a diva moment and tell them I would see them in court. I wouldn't have had a leg to stand on.

JF told me to take a seat. 'Darling, this is OK,' he said, in his heavy French accent. 'I don't blame you. I understand that you need to leave. This is ridiculous; I get it. You can't continue like this. You have to do this tour because it is good for you, and then you are going to do four solo albums.'

Four solo albums? I had no idea what he meant. 'I can't do four solo albums,' I replied. 'I didn't come here for that ...'

'No. You are going to honour your contract, which was for five albums: so you have done one album with Eternal, and now you are going to do four solo albums. You are going to be great. This is going to be fantastic. I just know it.'

Walking away, I realised that I had no say in this; it was going to happen. Frankly, I was stunned. I had never for a second thought that they would ask me to do a solo album, let alone four. I should have been jumping for joy, but I was afraid I wasn't good enough. It was all so bittersweet. I felt sad, because I had loved being part of the group and I've always been someone who much prefers being a small part of something huge rather than being a small part of something mediocre. I felt relieved that they had found a way for me to fulfil my contract, and I knew how lucky I was, but at the same time, I was filled with doubt. Could I be a success as a solo artist?

In those moments when everything seems to have gone wrong in my career, I have always managed to navigate myself towards the right person – or people – to help pull me up and move me forwards. JF obviously felt like I had a shot at a solo career, so I clung to his belief in me. Sometimes, when you're feeling low, it is hard to imagine that someone else can have faith in you. That they can see the strength and resilience within you, even when you've all but written yourself off. It might be a friend, a family member or even a colleague, but when they tell you that they believe in you – trust them.

Soon I was back with the Eternal girls, supporting Take That on their Nobody Else tour across Europe, performing at all the massive stadiums in Germany, Belgium, Switzerland, Brussels, Italy, Austria and the Netherlands. I think we were the only girl band that could've done that. We were proper tomboys – we were actually more boyish than they were. If we'd been a sexy girl band, I think we would've been ripped apart by the fans, but it was clear to everyone that we weren't trying to hit on the boys – we were all just friends. The Take That fans were pretty die-hard and the extremes they went to were just crazy. The screaming was ear-splitting and the hysteria and tears were an everyday occurrence as hordes of fans waited to catch a glimpse of the boys as they left venues or hotels.

For the first time, I didn't feel lonely when I was away,

because I was allowed to take someone with me. At first, my boyfriend at the time came along, but he went home quite quickly because it didn't work out. There was a moment when he was making a model aeroplane in my dressing room and I just thought, 'This isn't working.' So a friend came along with me instead, and we had such a laugh.

The Take That boys were great and we all had a brilliant time. Weirdly, as the tour went on, the mood seemed better between me and the other Eternal girls – everyone just seemed calmer and more relaxed. I think seeing how the boys behaved showed us how things could've been, and made us realise that touring didn't need to be so regulated. The boys all had their own lives and had girlfriends and family with them – and it worked. In our free time, everyone would go off and have time out, and then we could all come back together. For the first time since I had started in Eternal, I didn't feel so cut off. I got really friendly with Rob (Robbie Williams), who was going through something similar to me and was finding being on the road tough. The boys would often book a club or bar in whatever town we were in, and invite us and all the crew along. On the nights we performed, I would watch the boys' show from the sound deck because it was the best spot. I knew their show as well as they did. We would always make our 'getaway' by leaving five minutes before them to avoid the huge scrum of fans who congregated behind the gates.

As we travelled from one venue to another, I knew

that I was leaving the group at the end of the tour. I was so proud of what we'd achieved, but my time with Eternal had come to an end, and I was ready to embrace a new start. I had made the decision: it was time to see it through.

You've Got This ...

You are always good enough – never let anyone make you think that you are anything less

There have been times in my life, at the height of my fame, when I couldn't even move without a security guard shadowing me – but I've also had times where I could go and do my shopping in the supermarket or pop out to buy a pint of milk like any other person. It's taught me what fame is really about – and it certainly doesn't make you better than anyone else. We're all just humans with our own lives and challenges. For me, singing and performing is a job, and I take fame with a pinch of salt. Celebrity can really change people, but that machine can only churn for so long. Over the years, I've seen people come and go: one day, someone can be everywhere and on the front of every magazine and newspaper; then a year or even a few months later, no one is interested in them. I always find it amusing that on the front row of some of the shows at London and Paris fashion weeks, there are always some people that look so impressed with themselves. I can't help thinking, *If only you knew that in three years' time, you won't be invited. Don't look down on those people sitting a few rows behind you.*

Do you ever feel like an imposter?

Imposter syndrome is the feeling that your success is fake or undeserved, and that you might get 'caught out' at any moment for not being the 'real thing'. When I was in Eternal, from the outside it must have looked like I was living the dream – and in some ways, I was – but I always felt 'less than'. If only I'd maintained that feeling of confidence that I had when I was at school, when I really believed in myself. There were lots of things that were said and done during my time in Eternal. I never stood up for myself, and I take my share of the blame for that. I wish I'd been more open about how I felt. When one of the girls said something to upset me, I wish I'd spoken out more and challenged them. I felt like it didn't matter if I was there or not, and I allowed this situation to continue. So it wasn't just their fault – it was mine, too. It wasn't even like I was comparing myself to the other girls. I just didn't value my own contribution enough. I worked so hard, but never gave myself enough credit.

Always address your feelings

The feeling of never being 'good enough' has also been a feature in my romantic relationships. When I was married, I honestly got to the stage that when I walked into a room with Jamie, I felt like other people were surprised that he had chosen me and was still with me. I had this idea that everyone expected him to be with a six-foot-tall blonde model. I wasn't that person and I was never going to be. It just goes to show that these feelings can creep into every part of our lives. We all experience feelings like this at times, but what's important is trying to understand *why* we feel like this way – and then trying to do something about it. I don't think we tend to suffer from imposter syndrome when we're sitting on the sofa at home. Instead, it hits us in those moments when we are surrounded by other people who may not know or understand us. In my career – and my relationships – I just wished I'd addressed it and said how I really felt. I wish I'd owned it a bit more and had those important conversations. In the band, I should've told the other girls I was every bit as important as them. I should've had more boundaries and been more aware of my own worth, and I shouldn't have let the way I felt be dictated so much by others. In the same situation now, I think I would have handled these issues quite differently; I would've been much more assertive and not allowed the low blows to hit. And when it comes to relationships, I never want to feel like I am not good enough for someone. The minute we have these kinds of thoughts, we must address them. If we leave them to fester, they become debilitating.

Insecurity is all part of being human

In some ways, I think experiencing insecurity can be a good thing, as it forces us to grow and change. We all have those times where we don't feel good enough; be it as a parent, in our work, or in our relationships. It's not even always about the big stuff. When I am reading social media comments, for example, I will never focus on the ten good comments – it will always be the one negative one that gets me, and it can really hurt. Small things like that can really throw me off. I try to tell myself that as long as I am living with integrity and trying hard, it does not matter what other people think. We can't control the people around us, especially difficult people – we can only control how we respond to them. Now, when someone says something negative to me, I try to think, *What they are saying is not really about me at all; it is about them and their own issues.* Your feelings and ideas belong to you, so never allow anyone else to invalidate them. Surround yourself with positive and passionate people who bring out the best in you.

It is how you talk to yourself that matters most

Sometimes we can look at ourselves through the wrong kind of lens: one that seems to amplify our imperfections. You need to love yourself, no matter what, and you don't need to be perfect or some kind of superwoman to earn love from yourself or anyone else. Think about how you talk to yourself and question whether you would talk to someone else in that way. We tend to judge ourselves extremely harshly, whether we are aware of it or not, because we are conditioned to behave or look a certain way. It is very easy to slip into negative self-talk, and sometimes I find myself doing this without even realising it. Try to put a halt to any negative internal thought patterns and treat yourself with love and care. If you're having a bad day, shrug it off and know that you can start afresh tomorrow. The world will keep turning, and it's always OK to give yourself a break. No one has to be their 'best self' twenty-four hours a day, regardless of what Instagram might lead us to believe. By constantly pushing ourselves to be something else, or something better, we end up exhausted. Just be you.

Life is imperfect, but that doesn't mean you should lower the bar for what you'd like to do or achieve

No one else can decide what is important to you. When you know your worth is equal to everyone else's, it allows you to pursue your dreams and enjoy your life. Do this on your own terms.

Chapter Three

SUCCESS CAN COME
IN LOTS OF WAYS

'Success comes from knowing that you did your best to become the best that you are capable of becoming.'

John Wooden

Reclining in beige, leather-clad loungers, my manager Wendy and I clinked champagne glasses. We were on a ten-seater private jet, flying to Marrakesh to do a shoot for *FHM*.

'Anything I can get for you ladies?' asked the flight attendant.

'We're good, thanks,' I replied. I mean, what more could we have wanted?

On the flight, there was quite a lot of turbulence. During one particularly rocky wave, Wendy's drink shot out of her glass, and she tried her very best to catch every last drop of it. 'Better not waste the good stuff!' she laughed.

Looking back at moments like that reminds me of just how much fun I've had in my career. At the time, I had started doing more and more shoots for *FHM*. Shooting for them was a bit of an ego boost, and I was pretty surprised that men were so interested in me – it was the first proper male attention I'd had in my life. I wasn't quite sure how Louise from Lewisham had got to the point where she was being flown around in private jets. Although my life had changed so much, I still felt like a normal girl – just one whose career was going pretty well. I guess I hadn't quite grasped the level of my success, so it all felt quite surreal.

Back then, *FHM* was one of the most popular men's magazines out there. I was no longer quite as naïve as when I'd started out, so I always knew that they would require some quite sexy photos. The thought of trying to look sexy did play on my mind, but I was happy to go with the flow as long as the photos were tasteful and respectful. More often than not, I insisted on wearing a sarong over the top of my bikini. I know that some people thought the pictures were quite sleazy, but I made sure that the shoots were always within my comfort zone and I actually found them quite empowering and fun.

Nowadays, I think you could be ribbed or even slightly judged for posing for magazine covers wearing swimwear or lingerie, but back then, it felt like a real compliment to be asked. Some people say it was sexist, but I think it really celebrated and empowered women. Some of the magazine covers of that time are really iconic and featured people like Madonna, Jennifer Lopez and Halle Berry. My rule for shoots was simple: if my nan and Grandad Malcolm couldn't be proud of the photos and put them in their scrapbook, then I wouldn't do it. They were my biggest fans, and everything I ever did, they collected; every newspaper or magazine cutting; every picture; every album – it was all there. During Eternal, and then during my solo career, I did a lot of TV, but if Mum or I forgot to ring and tell them I was going to be on the telly, I would get a call from my nan saying, 'My neighbour Joan had to tell me you were on *GMTV*. I am so embarrassed! How could I not know this, Lou? You've got to keep me up to date with what you are doing.'

By then, Nan and Grandad Malcolm had given up running pubs and had retired to Tunbridge Wells in Kent, so if I was ever performing in theatre-type venues, I always pushed for Tunbridge Wells to be on the list so they didn't have a long journey home. Their opinion has always been incredibly important to me, so I owed it to them – and to myself – to make sure every shoot was scrapbook-appropriate. There was one *FHM* shoot where I wore a black lacy lingerie set. When I look at it now, I think, *How did they manage to get me into that?* I'm not sure that one made it into the scrapbook. I think it is so important to know when to stand your ground. Sometimes it can be easier to go along with what everyone else wants from you, but then you can end up compromising on what you believe in, and you may find yourself in a situation that you don't feel comfortable with. I never said yes to wearing anything that I didn't want to. When I was asked to wear swimwear for a shoot, I would say that was fine, as long as the shoot was on a beach or by a pool. I would have looked like a right wally if I was posing in swimwear in a random bedroom. And I'm glad that I always made a point of that. In your career, particularly when you're starting out, 'No' can often feel like this awful, taboo word. There is a lazy assumption that if you are asking for something, especially as a woman, that you're being difficult. But learning to understand your limits and knowing when to say no is such an important skill.

Arriving in Marrakesh on that trip, we tried to shoot the pictures on the beach, but we soon put paid to that idea as it became apparent that we would be arrested. Women are not allowed to be scantily clad in public over there, and that includes what we would see as beachwear. We tried taking some shots of me walking down the cobbled lanes in a white crochet dress with a bikini underneath instead, and people started shouting and hollering at us that they were going to call the police. The picture editor obviously hadn't thought that one through. We ended up shooting a lot of the pictures at a hotel and around the pool, and these photos are still some of my absolute favourites. They were just revealing enough, but mainly they were elegant and cool.

Looking back, that time was an incredible flurry of

magazine covers, big music videos and massive live performances on stage. I worked so, so hard, but I had turned a corner. My solo career had taken off, and I was having the best time of my life.

x x x

Leaving Eternal was such a leap of faith. I had been really worried that no one would buy my records and that the fans would hate me for leaving, but overall it was such a positive transition, and my fans were – and always have been – such superstars.

When I left the group, I started working with Simon Climie from Climie Fisher, who was a big songwriter, and the first single we released was a ballad called 'Light of My Life'. When the record company told me that this was going to be my first single, I thought they were crazy. By this stage, I understood the record industry enough to know that this was a risk – no one releases a ballad as a first single – but it was a great song. I remember the week it came out; I was in the car when Denis called with news of the chart position. I was so nervous and scared. I kept saying to him, 'Don't tell me, I don't want to know.' But when he said it was number three in the midweek charts, I screamed my head off. I was so happy. It felt like all of my hard work and perseverance were finally paying off. When you are in a difficult situation and forced to make a life-changing decision, it can be overwhelming. It's easy to start wondering if you made the right choice, but I think it's important to always be true to how you feel and to go with your gut. That way, you can live without looking back and thinking about what might have been. And when you push yourself out of your comfort zone, it often comes good.

My press agent felt like we needed to move away from the image I'd had in Eternal, so I went and did a shoot with an incredible fashion photographer called Mario Sorrenti, who was a regular for magazines like *Vogue* and *Harper's Bazaar*. He was famous for the incredible Calvin Klein shot of Kate Moss lying naked on the sofa. My experience of photoshoots for Eternal had been full-on. Even though we wore casual clothes, we also wore loads of make-up, and our hair was always heavily styled to the extent that it could have lasted for days. This guy had the biggest hair and make-up people in the world on speed dial, and this was a time when you earned thousands of pounds for a day's shoot, so I was expecting the full works.

'Just wet her hair and put it in a knot. She just needs black eyeliner and a jumper,' he said.

There were no lights, and I just sat on the floor. And that was the single cover for 'Light of My Life'. I had no idea what was going on or what it would look like. Now I realise how lucky I was to work with one of the biggest fashion photographers of that era.

Music videos were also massive back then, and we did this huge video with four big scenes in it. We booked Hawaii for the beach shoot, forgetting about the black sand – I looked like I was rolling around in mud for most of the video! But I still remember someone saying to me, 'Whatever you do, make sure you don't take any of the volcanic ash with you, because it's bad luck.'

Unfortunately, I was wearing exactly the kind of shoes that meant all the sand got caught in the heels. As I was packing, I was desperately trying to brush all the sand off them. Maybe it's just an old superstition, but when we were flying home there was really bad turbulence, and I was absolutely convinced someone had brought back some of the sand in their luggage. In the end, we decided to go to LA to shoot some cutaway scenes. I was slightly nervous about being jinxed. On one Australian TV show, I performed in two left shoes after I picked up the wrong ones from a shop. A few weeks later in Germany, I was performing with four dancers in blue velvet trouser suits when, during the last number, we all heard simultaneous rips as our bums were exposed to an audience of record company execs!

By this stage, I loved my work, because I got on brilliantly with everyone I worked with. My radio promoter, my producers, my hairdresser, my make-up artists, and all the other people around me became like a second family. To this day, I still work with the same hairdresser that shot my very first music video and the same TV plugger, Jacqui Quaife, and radio promoter, Carrie Curtis, that I had during the Eternal years. In fact, I'm so close to my hairdresser, Bill Currie, that he's even sat outside some of my therapy appointments over the years. Because I had made or was making these lifelong friends, it never felt like a job, despite working so hard and being back on a packed music-making and promotion schedule. I was also learning that things didn't need to be the way they'd been with Eternal. It was possible to work really, really hard without having to spend weeks and weeks away from home. I was discovering that I could build myself up slowly as an artist. When I was with Eternal, we were told what to say, what to do, what to think, so it took me a while to learn to have my own opinions.

I always knew that I had a lot to live up to. One thing I had learned by that point was that you are only as big as your last record. Ultimately, the harsh truth was that, even if everyone was my friend, if I wasn't selling music, I would get dropped, and that would be the end of my career. So I knew that I had to keep going and keep making a success of it. It made me dig deep and give everything my absolute all.

A turning point that changed the course of my career was my 1996 track 'Naked', which was the third single that I released. I worked with a choreographer called Jamie King on the video; he is incredible and has worked with huge, huge names like Madonna, Michael Jackson and Diana Ross, so I had very big shoes to fill. The video was shot in a warehouse in LA, and I was given this white outfit to wear. I walked into a room with a chaise longue bang in the middle, and Jamie said, 'Right, we're going to start like this, with your hands together above your head.'

What is this? I was thinking. *I really am on my own now!*

Much to my relief, the shoot went brilliantly. There had been a conscious effort to recast my image from the young girl in Eternal to a slightly sultrier, more grown-up look, and this video did a great job of that. At first, if someone told me to be 'sexy', I found it quite hard, as that's not how I naturally saw myself; I've always been the smiley girl. But I've found that sexiness doesn't have to mean trying to look seductive – for me, it's confidence and owning the moment.

As I've said, I'm always at my happiest and most confident when I'm performing. The days spent touring, writing music and singing live made me come alive, and there were many, many good times. One of my favourite events to attend was the annual *Smash Hits* awards. I was a girl in pop, so while this might not have been the BAFTAs or the Oscars, winning an award still felt like a real accolade and something that every artist aimed for. There was one year where I had been performing, so I was mainly backstage, but I kept coming out from the wings to collect the various awards that I'd won. When it came to my fifth award, Ant and Dec, who were presenting, started to joke that I needed a wheelbarrow to carry everything home that day. That recognition really meant the world to me and was such a confidence boost. I was so grateful for my incredible fans, who had lifted me up and kept me going.

x x x

Things were also moving in a new direction in my personal life. Robbie Williams introduced me to Jamie while we were touring with Take That. Rob said, 'You must meet my mate.' I thought he was just a young football player who was asking me for my number. Did I think I had met my future husband? Definitely not. I had only had one proper relationship before Jamie. That had lasted about three years, and I don't think I was any sort of girlfriend. I had worked all the time and was never there for Christmases, birthdays or New Year's Eves – I was always working, so I'm not surprised that it didn't work out. We were also really young. It wasn't a big break-up – the relationship just ran its course.

The first time I met Jamie was after one of the Take That performances. All of those big stadiums have these huge underground areas, and there I was in my kneepads, shorts, a Puffa jacket, massive socks and Timberland boots after our performance.

'So, when someone asked me who my celebrity crush was recently in an interview, I said it was you,' he said, with a grin on his face.

'I'm not sure this is what you were expecting,' I replied, pointing down to my very casual outfit.

Maybe I was not what Jamie had imagined, but we soon struck up an easy friendship. Of course, he was very good-looking, but I knew he was young and probably not ready for a serious relationship, and I didn't want to be messed about. I was quite single-minded about my work, so I wasn't going to jump into anything unless it felt right. I thought we were better off as mates at that stage, and it worked.

We would hang out together when we could. We were both very busy with our respective careers, but there was always the odd evening or day which we both had free. There were so many things I liked about Jamie, including the fact that he rang his mum every day. I am incredibly close to my family, so I could see he was a good guy when he did that. By then, I had a flat in Fulham and he was playing for Liverpool, but we would spend time together when he was in London. I remember one time he was going on holiday with his mates to Ayia Napa and he asked me to pick up a few things for him, as I was recording in town and he planned to come over in the evening. It hit me that I didn't want him to go away, and as he left, I felt really quite upset. I wasn't stupid – I knew what those sort of boys' holidays probably entailed – and it was clear to me that I was starting to have feelings for him. And he'd hinted that it was the same for him. If I had a date, he'd ask, 'Oh, who with?' I felt slightly possessive over him, and I think he felt the same about me.

After the holiday, Jamie came straight from the airport to my flat, and I think we both knew from there that it was no longer just a friendship. Our first date that night was to an Italian restaurant. I remember taking about three hours deciding what to wear, trying on about twenty-five outfits. It was one of those restaurants where the walls are covered with framed black-and-white pictures of all the famous people who have been there.

For the entire evening, I stared at a picture of Jamie and some friends, with his arm around a girl. When we got home, I asked him who the girl was. He laughed. 'I was hoping that you weren't going to notice that!' he said.

Around a year later, Jamie broke his ankle during a game. He was devastated, and I just knew that I wanted to be with him, so I went straight to the hospital and ending up spending five days there while he was recuperating. That time we spent together is what cemented us. I understood his passion for what he did. He was hungry for his work and I understood that feeling, because I felt the same about my own career.

Towards the end of that hospital stay, we were sitting in his room and he said to me, 'I think we should probably get married, then.'

It wasn't the most romantic proposal, and I think we even had a silly row afterwards when I told him he shouldn't have proposed just because he felt it was the right thing to do. I mean, only *I* could've accepted a proposal in that way! But we were happy, and the wheels were set in motion for us to tie the knot.

We had started looking at different wedding venues in the UK, thinking we'd have a big ceremony, but in the end, we got married while we were on holiday in Bermuda. All over Bermuda, there are these special arches and when I asked someone what they were, they told me about the national symbol, called 'the Moongate'. They're all over the island, and Bermudan legend says that if you walk through one holding hands, you will be blessed with eternal love and happiness. On the spur of the moment, we decided to get married there, on a boat underneath one of these special arches. It was really low-key with just my family, Jamie's family and a couple of friends who flew out to be with us.

Both of us were still working hard, so sometimes finding enough time together was tough. My singing and performing schedule was full on, and Jamie was at Liverpool. A lot of my jobs were in London or other big cities, so I spent a lot of time on trains or standing on the platform at Euston station. Some days, I would finish work at six or seven o'clock in the evening and catch the train up to Liverpool to spend the night with Jamie, before catching the train back to London at eight o'clock the next morning and heading back into the studio for the day. I didn't mind, though; the long hours travelling were definitely worth it for a few hours together.

Our first proper house that we bought together was a small section of a converted barn in Heswall. After a year or so, I was able to take some time out after releasing the album *Elbow Beach*. For a few months, I enjoyed being in the house and just being with Jamie. I loved being a 'proper' wife, rather than a part-time one, which is how I'd felt until that point. I was able to cook dinner and make our house into a home. However, something shifted inside me. I don't know whether it was because of taking this time out from my career, but I'm not sure I ever really fully regained my confidence afterwards. I did head back into the industry, but I found it harder than before. I was less self-assured. It was as though I had taken my foot off the pedal, and now it was harder to keep moving forwards in the same way. There were new people on the block, which made it feel tough. Looking back, I wish I'd celebrated my achievements and successes more.

You've Got This . . .

Think about how you measure success? What does success mean to you? Do you consider yourself to be successful?

Success is a pretty magical word, and one with huge connotations. I guess we all want to be and feel successful in whatever we do, and it's something we all strive for. It's always a great feeling when hard work pays off. During my early twenties, I learned that professional success comes in many different forms. Back then, I wanted to be seen as a serious and credible music artist, but it didn't mean I couldn't also be on the front of magazines. No one should be put into one box. You can do many things and be successful at them all.

When we look at social media, we see a very narrow definition of success

When we see people online who have huge homes, amazing careers, high-profile relationships, supermodel bodies, or vast social media followings, we automatically class them as being successful. Rarely do we look beyond the pictures and question whether that person has a great character, whether they have fulfilling personal relationships, or if they are actually happy. We tend to make a snap judgement about what we see on the surface: we look at them and assume they are 'all set' in life. No one ever considers what personal battles these people may be facing, whether in their careers, their relationships or in other parts of their lives. You only know what it looks like from the outside. Many people who struggle to get to where they are actually end up burned out and unhappy, but no one reveals that sort of stuff on Instagram.

Follow your passions – if you can do that, you are winning

True success cannot just be about making money, it has to be about doing something that you truly love; something that makes you tick. I know how lucky I am that what I love to do has paid financial rewards, but this cannot be the be-all and end-all. It is important to look at life and identify where your passions lie. Having a career isn't the only marker of success. I know that I am at my happiest when I'm performing, and also when I'm with my kids. Always follow your passion, whether it's your career, your family, your friendships, your creativity or something else.

Comparing ourselves to others is human nature, but that doesn't mean it's healthy

All too often, we gauge our own success against that of other people and what they are doing. In a way, it's human nature: we all want to measure our success somehow, and this is the most obvious way. I have been guilty of this all my life, even when I'm not making a conscious decision to look at what other people are doing. If something good happens to me, I tend to compare it with another person and what they are up to. Many women I know do the same, even if we don't always admit it. I think, in general, that women are more susceptible to this than men because our society so often pits us against each other. It's like there are only so many seats at the table, so competition is key to our professional success. But no one else's win is a loss for you. If looking at other people's lives inspires you, that's great – but when it starts to make you feel bad, it's time to step away.

How can we free ourselves from this culture of comparison?

Not only is comparison unhelpful, it's also unfair and unrealistic to compare yourself to someone else. Every person and every situation is unique. In order to free ourselves from this culture of comparison, we need to remember to frequently unplug from social media and see it for what it really is: the highlights reel of someone's life, not reality. We see what they want us to see, not the whole truth. Do not be tricked into thinking that you're the only one facing an uphill battle. What I am learning (and it's something I would love to try to do more) is that we need to gauge our successes against our own achievements and abilities, not those of others. Focus on what *you* have done professionally and what *you* have overcome on a personal level. Set goals that'll help you achieve what *you* want. For me, success is about doing your best, even if it doesn't lead to big results. I want to write the music that is real to me now, and while I hope to make music that people want to listen to, I also want to be true to myself. When I released my album *Heavy Love*, I knew I had poured my heart and soul into it, and that mattered far more to me than how many copies it sold.

While professional accomplishments form one piece of the puzzle, there are so many others

Do you enjoy your work? Are you healthy? Are you happy? Everyone has different ideas about what success is, and it's important to remember that there is no right or wrong answer. The best way to achieve success is to define what it means for you and then build your goals accordingly. It's OK to listen to and accept the definitions of success that others give us, but ultimately we are the only ones who can really decide whether we are successful. For some people, it might be having a steady nine-to-five job that allows them to fulfil other passions; for others it may be travelling. Personally, I see success as balancing my love of what I do with having meaningful relationships with my family and friends. Most importantly, my children will always come first, regardless of anything else. Ultimately, success is about living the life that you want, whether you desire professional success or prefer to seek happiness and fulfilment from other parts of your life. However you see success, it shouldn't need recognition from the rest of the world (or on social media!).

Always trust yourself first and know that you can create a successful life, no matter how you define it. I love this quote from Maya Angelou: 'Success is liking yourself, liking what you do, and liking how you do it.' This is so true – just be you.

Chapter Four

TRUST YOURSELF
AS A MOTHER

'Motherhood ... all love begins and ends there.'
Robert Browning

I woke up from the anaesthetic feeling groggy and light-headed. The first person I saw when I opened my eyes was Dr Silverstone, my silver-haired gynaecologist, who was sitting on the end of my bed at Portland Hospital. I had just had a procedure called a laparoscopy, in which the surgeon had made an incision into my belly button in order to look around my abdomen with a camera.

'Right, my darling, we need to talk.' Dr Silverstone is a slim older gentleman and has the most reassuring and comforting tone, but this wasn't what I was expecting to hear.

'What do you mean?' I asked.

'Before I start, I want to tell you not to worry – we will sort it out. What we have found is endometriosis.'

I am sure a lot of you already know, but endometriosis is a condition where tissue which is similar to the lining of the womb starts to grow elsewhere in your abdomen. He told me that my womb was facing the wrong way, and my bowel had become attached to it because of the extra tissue that had been growing. I had been on the pill for a long time, but had stopped taking it a few years earlier. My periods had returned to normal, but I'd been experiencing severe lower back pain (which I was convinced was due to having spent a lot of time standing in the studio and being very active) and I hadn't got pregnant.

'Am I going to be able to have children?' I asked nervously, already sensing that his reply might not be what I wanted to hear.

'I don't know,' he said. 'There will definitely be some hurdles to overcome, and it might be tough, but I promise we will do everything we can to help you have a family.'

My heart sank. Jamie wasn't with me that day, as I'd convinced myself that the test would show that nothing was wrong, so instead my mum came in and held my hand as we talked to Dr Silverstone about what we could do next and how we would overcome it.

As he walked out of the room, I felt a tremendous sense of guilt: what if this was my fault?

In the early days after we got married, I didn't feel

ready for children, even though Jamie wanted them straight away. I understood that he wanted his kids to see him play football, and because footballers' careers are so short, time was ticking by with every year. But I wasn't ready to be a mum and make all the career sacrifices that come with having a baby and raising a family. I never said, 'I don't want kids,' out loud. I just hoped that it wouldn't happen – and it didn't, even after I came off the pill. Every month that went by and I wasn't pregnant, I felt the same sense of relief wash over me. I never told a soul how I felt – I was worried I was being unbelievably selfish. At that point, everyone was talking all the time about us having kids and hearing the patter of tiny feet, and I would just smile, laugh, and say nothing. I felt like the questions came from every direction, completely unprompted.

In the early stages, I just brushed it off, but after a few years had elapsed and I still wasn't pregnant, Jamie became concerned. I still thought it was nothing and that the doctors would tell me everything was fine. We were both busy and travelling a lot for work. I went for the tests just to shut everyone up, fully expecting the doctors to tell us to keep trying because getting pregnant is not always that easy, and that it would happen at the right time. So, when I was told that I might not be able to have children, it immediately felt like it was my fault – as if, somehow, by not wanting children early on, I had tempted fate. I was devastated.

I stood outside the hospital and called Jamie. It was

one of the hardest conversations I have ever had to have. I was almost lost for words, struggling to explain what had happened and what Dr Silverstone had told me. Jamie was very quiet at the end of the phone, but he reassured me, saying we would sort it out and it would be all right. I thought of all the things that a wife was supposed to give her husband – if I couldn't have children, would I feel like I was depriving him of a family? Despite my own career success, my self-confidence was shaky at this time, and this felt like another huge hit.

It was probably at this point that my insecurities about not being good enough started to spiral. Jamie is a successful, good-looking and wealthy sportsman, and I felt like he could've married any girl he wanted to. I had always had great relationships with other women, but for the first time, I started to notice that some women don't appear to acknowledge that a man is married or has a girlfriend. Everywhere we went, glamorous and gorgeous women tried to get Jamie's attention. They would sidle over to him in clubs, flicking their hair, all dolled up in their heels and tight dresses. It was like I was invisible to these women – or maybe they just didn't care. Either way, I started to feel even less confident in myself and what I had to offer Jamie.

x x x

Despite this terrifying diagnosis, I had one thing in my favour. I had always been quite healthy, eating well and

keeping fit. Looking back, I can see that I had a cracking body with a flat stomach; I wish I had been more
proud of it back then. I always enjoy a drink and love
the occasional good night out, but I've never done drugs
or been remotely interested in them. Back in the day,
drugs were commonplace in the music industry, and it
was completely normal to see someone smoking weed
or snorting coke off the nearest table. Seeing at first hand
the effects drugs had on the people around me put me
right off from the start. I didn't see anyone become ill,
but the drugs would often turn them into a sweaty mess.
So I would much prefer to have a new pair of shoes than
a line of coke. To be honest, I was fortunate, as I was able
to get a natural high from performing.

Although logically I knew that the endometriosis
wasn't my fault, it was still hard to shake that feeling
of guilt. I was really, really scared that I had somehow
ruined our chances of having a family. After we had
come to terms with my diagnosis, I was prescribed
hormones that would bring on the start of the menopause; the idea being that this would slow down the
endometriosis. It meant that I had to inject myself with
hormones every day, which wasn't a particularly pleas-
ant experience. But by this point, I was so desperate to
have kids, I was willing to try anything. So I sucked it
up and followed my doctor's advice to a tee, doing my
best to manage the horrible hormonal side effects. My
mum was going through menopause herself, and we
would sit in the car together, both having hot flushes

and fanning our faces at the same time. It was all right for her – I wasn't supposed to be having hot flushes at my age!

Ironically, the best thing to ease endometriosis is pregnancy, but that hadn't happened for me, so I had to get on with the treatment. I knew that I couldn't keep blaming myself and feeling down about it all, so I tried to change my mindset. I became completely determined to do everything I could to give us the best chance of having a family. Of course, all our close family and friends were quite careful not to say too much, as they knew what was going on behind the scenes, but people who didn't know us well would still always ask when we were planning on having a baby. The subject would crop up in interviews without fail, and it was increasingly hard to field the questions. It used to make me really tearful, and I would have to bite my lip. I know it's a pretty innocent question, but as anyone with fertility issues will know, it can be a horrible one to have to answer. I think I went into 'PR Louise' mode, which involved me trotting out the same generic reply or just smiling and not saying much. I was at the height of my solo career and *FHM* days when I was told I might not be able to have children, and while I felt on top of the world with my career, the pregnancy struggle was bruising. In a way, it felt like some of my femininity had been taken from me, and I had a sense that I had completely underachieved – a feeling that I am not good at dealing with, even at the best of times. On the outside, it looked like I was living a perfect life, but like everyone, I had my private battles.

In the end, I had two operations to laser away the extra tissue and remove everything from my womb. I was lucky enough to be able to take some time out to recover. After that, we were just told to try again and see what happened. The problem with endometriosis is that there isn't really a permanent cure – even once you have removed the tissue, it starts to grow back again, making a natural pregnancy more difficult. We were all aware that the longer it took, the harder it would be. I had the final operation in the summer. We made the decision that we would give ourselves a bit of time to try to fall pregnant naturally, and then we would start the IVF process in December.

I found out I was pregnant in November, on the same day that my Grandad Charlie died. He was in a home by this stage after suffering a stroke, and he was not the man he used to be. The man I had known during my childhood, who had once been the life and soul of the market, was no longer really recognisable. The smart Crombie coat and cravat had been swapped for slippers and a jumper. Whenever I visited him, I felt quite emotional, as we struggled to chat the way we once had. It is always hard to see someone so vibrant become so frail.

I had noticed that morning that my period was a few days late. Mum happened to be at my house, so I was having a chat with her about it. She told me it would be better to know for sure rather than speculate, so she popped out to the shops to buy a test, which we were both expecting to be negative. I gave it to Mum to read because the wait was making me anxious; it is such an excruciating process trying not to stare at the stick. I couldn't believe it when she told me there were two blue lines. I think because I knew we were going to start having IVF soon, I had relaxed and all the stress dissipated. I just sat on the stairs in disbelief.

As we waited for Jamie to come home from training – I wanted to make sure I told him in person – we got the call to tell us that Grandad Charlie had died. My emotions were all over the place. I felt so desperately sad about the loss of Grandad, but part of me was also relieved that he wouldn't have to suffer any more. He was so different to the man he had been in his prime, and I knew he must have hated struggling to communicate and look after himself. I also felt an overwhelming sense of joy and apprehension about finally being pregnant. Somehow, it felt like my grandad had chosen to make space for my baby. I think he thought, *It's Lou's turn now.*

As soon as I'd told Jamie about the positive test, I phoned Dr Silverstone. We were all quite nervous, as by this time it felt like we had all been through a lot together. His secretary, Gemma, had also been there with us every step of the way. She arranged for me to go in for some tests and a scan.

When Dr Silverstone finally confirmed that yes, I was definitely pregnant, we all welled up – me, Jamie and the doctor. It felt like we had finally hit the jackpot after months of gruelling treatment and uncertainty about the future. Like every first-time mum, I was very nervous about what I needed to do and what would happen next, and I had so many questions. I was lucky to have such an amazing doctor, and he reassured me that he would be by my side throughout the process. Dr Silverstone has spent years and years delivering babies, but by then he had turned his attention to gynaecology more generally. He was so supportive, though, and because he knew how much I trusted him, he promised that he would deliver my baby regardless.

When I was sixteen weeks pregnant, we had a scan to find out the sex of the baby. Being a typical sportsman, Jamie was desperate for a boy. When we were told that we were indeed having a boy, it felt amazing.

Throughout my first pregnancy, I suffered from really bad morning sickness for the whole nine months. I felt so horrendous that I decided to take some time off, as I really wasn't up to doing much. I had really mixed emotions about stopping work. Having worked so hard from such a young age, I was loving having a normal life. Something as simple as going to the shops to buy a pint of milk was a novelty. It is hard to explain without sounding like a prick, but I hadn't really experienced what it was like to do a supermarket shop or sit out in the garden with a cup of tea. My time had always been completely mapped out because of my demanding schedule, so not having that was so refreshing.

Getting the house ready for the baby was so much fun. Small things, like decorating the nursery and picking out a cot and furniture, choosing the right pushchair and buying some gorgeous tiny outfits, filled me with joy. It was such an exciting and thrilling time, and buying the things our little one would need was part of that. I think it felt particularly important to me because for so long I'd thought it would never happen.

For the first time ever, we could make plans to be at home, or go to see friends in the evenings. When I was working, if anyone had asked if I could meet up or go over to theirs for dinner, I always had to check my diary. Nine times out of ten, I wouldn't be able to make it because of work commitments. It was honestly just so nice to feel like I was in control of my time again.

When I was eight months pregnant, I was named *FHM*'s 'Sexiest Woman of the Decade'. I wore a green dress to the awards ceremony and looked like a giant Granny Smith apple – probably not quite what they had in mind when they chose me! Years later, when I moved into my new house after my divorce, my friend Lewis made me put the award in my downstairs loo, but I always put it face down when anyone comes over – especially the boys' friends!

When I was pregnant with Charley, and then later when I had Beau, I suffered from hyperpigmentation, known as chloasma. I developed large dark patches around my forehead and cheeks. I don't think it helped that I spent so much time in the sun, even though I wore

Author's collection

My grandad Charlie helped me from start to finish with what I wanted to do in life.

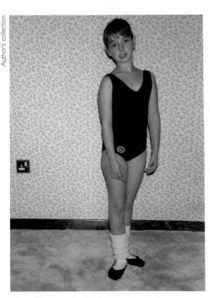

Author's collection

Me taking my ballet lessons very seriously . . . 3rd position.

Author's collection

Being able to see my mum get married was so special and I remember being so incredibly happy for her.

Author's collection

My first day at Conti's – and I was beyond excited.

Author's collection

Studio 45 where I spent most of my school days.
You couldn't get me out of dance class.

Author's collection

One of our first gigs as Eternal and I was just loving life . . .
I've still got those knee pads!

Author's collection

The day I met my true icon.

Author's collection

While I was pregnant I really suffered with skin pigmentation, but I didn't care because I was just so excited to meet my boy.

Author's collection

I've always been close to my family and shared lots of memorable times with my brothers, Joe and Sam.

Author's collection

Me with Charley. I still try and get a kiss on those cheeks even now he is so big.

Author's collection

My favourite time is when I escape somewhere with my boys, Charley and Beau. It makes me truly happy.

Author's collection

Doing *Strictly* with Daisy was so much fun. She's always smiling.

Author's collection

I haven't met many close friends in this business but in Rob I've truly found one.

Author's collection

With one of my closest friends, Charli. She's always been a real strength and a true friend.

Author's collection

Author's collection

Playing Sally Bowles in *Cabaret* was such an achievement for me. It had been over fifteen years since I had been on stage.

One of my favourite places to be creative – the studio.

© Kasia Clarke

I think the smile on my face says it all.

© Kasia Clarke

Filming the *Stretch* video. Being on that set was the first time in so many years that I felt confident enough in myself.

Author's collection

My little partner in crime, Miss Amber D. We had the best time working together on *9 to 5: The Musical.*

Author's collection

Everyone in this picture has played a big part in me moving on and having a career.

sunscreen. Later on, I went to see a dermatologist to talk about getting it removed, and I had some treatment, but it still comes back even now. It's one of those things that never really bothered me at the time, though, as all I was thinking about was my little boy and our new life as a family of three.

It was decided that I would have a Caesarean. I was full of nerves. I don't think any woman can explain that feeling the day before you are booked in for a C-section, knowing that in twenty-four hours' time, a baby will be in your arms. I remember just lying there with Jamie by my side, while opera played in the background. Dr Silverstone was full of his normal charm and reassurance.

'It looks fantastic down here,' he said. 'Absolutely great. It's all going to plan. I'm admiring from here – it's all looking fantastic.'

When they put Charley in my arms, I remember thinking, 'What on earth do I do now?' It was like I wasn't entirely sure how I was supposed to feel. I just felt a bit numb. I was wheeled back up to my room. When my family came to visit me, I just directed them to the cot.

'He's in that,' I said, pointing at it, seeing the blurry form of a small baby wrapped in a blanket. 'He's over there.'

It was only when the midwives asked me a day after the birth if I wanted to take him to have a bath, and I reluctantly agreed, that something changed. I waddled down the corridor to the room that they used to bathe the babies, pushing the trolley containing Charley. I don't know what happened in those moments between leaving my bed and reaching that room, but I fell head over heels in love. After that, I didn't want to put him down. The midwives kept asking if I wanted them to take him away so I could have a rest, but I didn't want to let him out of my sight. I remember waking up and immediately asking the midwives to bring him back. From then on, he didn't leave my side. I knew I would protect him until the day I died. Every mum says it, but you really do live for your kids – and that bond is so special, there's nothing else like it.

I loved having Charley and cherished every moment when he was small. Because I had spent so long not knowing if I would ever be able to have kids, I felt so blessed. I don't think I did anything 'right': he slept in my bed, I didn't breastfeed and I didn't read the parenting manuals. Mums are judged in so many ways. I was told I was 'too posh to push' because I'd had a Caesarean. Of course, I'd actually had it because my womb was facing the wrong way, so it was the best option, but I didn't want to share that with the whole world – and nor did I feel the need to justify myself. As for breastfeeding, I had seen my mum really struggle when she was breast-feeding my brothers. She suffered from mastitis, where the breast tissue becomes inflamed, and she lost a lot of her hair. I remember seeing her crying because she was in so much pain, but she continued to breastfeed anyway. I think it was because she felt like it was the 'done thing', not because she really wanted to. Watching my mum go through that had put me off, and Jamie really wanted to be hands-on and help with the feeds, which is something I didn't want to take away from him, so bottle-feeding was the right choice for us.

Charley was a gorgeous baby, but he didn't sleep. I remember being up twelve times a night for a while because he refused to sleep in his own bed. In fact, both of my kids slept in my bed for their entire childhoods – but then, I slept in my mum's bed when I was small. I even remember my mum taking me to the doctor and telling her that I wouldn't sleep in my own bed. The doctor had told her not to worry; there would come a time when I was ready to sleep on my own.

People don't all parent in the same way – that would be impossible. How can there be a general rule of thumb for parenting? I've always said that mums should do what works for them and their children. I was never that parent that chopped up carrots and put them in a Tupperware pot for a day at the farm. I was always the Quavers mum, dishing up crisps in one hand and a carton of juice in the other.

Apart from my mum helping me on some days, I never had a nanny – and even to this day, I've never used a babysitter. Jamie was away quite a lot, so Mum would sometimes come to stay with me if we were on our own at home, and she'd babysit occasionally in the evenings so Jamie and I could go out for dinner.

I was so content. I just loved being at home with Charley, and adored organising birthday parties for him and later Beau. It always felt like the perfect excuse for a big celebration, and I would go completely over the top, spending a fortune. I loved doing it for everyone: not just the kids, but for their friends and our family, too. There was one year when I really went to town. Charley used to love going to Bocketts Farm Park to pet the animals and run around, so for his third birthday, I threw him a cowboy-themed party. I had cowboy plates, hats for every kid, and loads of themed food. We had a bunch of Shetland ponies in the garden, a petting zoo, an ice-cream van and caterers. That still wasn't enough for me: I wanted it to look like a proper ranch. I knew Jamie and all of my family would think that I had lost the plot if I told them what I was really doing, so I said I was going out to get some balloons, then drove around the local area, stopping at anywhere that looked remotely like a farm to ask if I could buy some hay bales. Eventually, I found some and manhandled them into the boot and backseat, taking them home before going back to pick up the rest. I was lucky: I had the money to do it, I only had Charley, and it gave me a sense of purpose. Watching all the kids running around and petting the animals was the best feeling. Charley was given a Superman outfit, which he put on straight away, and I can just see him now, eating ice cream with a massive grin on his face.

Beau's birthday is in the winter, so it wasn't always as easy to throw big parties for him, but I still always tried to do something special. His parties tended to be on a smaller scale anyway, as he has always been more into having a close-knit group of friends over rather than lots of people. Like a lot of mums, most of my weekends were spent taking the boys to their friends' birthday parties. On one occasion, one of Beau's best friends, a boy called Max, had a go-karting party. All the kids had to do a couple of laps of the track to get a medal. Beau was absolutely desperate for the medal, but too scared to drive the go-kart himself. In the end, he begged me to get into the kart and do the laps for him so he could get the medal. There I was, driving alongside a bunch of six-year-olds, bum squeezed into the seat. And I won! Beau was beside himself.

Charley was five when Beau was born, and for us it felt like the perfect gap between them, although of course I don't know any other way. I was in the swing of parenting by then. I'd had my special time with Charley and he was going off to school, so it felt right. I didn't feel sad when Charley went off in his little shorts and a blazer. He was so full of energy all the time, and I felt like he was really ready for the structure and stimulation of school.

When we started trying for another baby, I never thought it would happen so quickly. I was shocked to find that it only took me four weeks to fall pregnant. I had been on the pill, so my endometriosis had been managed by that, and I was very lucky. My doctor had told me that unless it happened quickly, it was likely I would have to go down the same route that I had done when we were trying for Charley, and we would've had to have IVF. So it was such a wonderful surprise.

When I was pregnant with Beau, it was a very similar experience to my first pregnancy. I suffered from morning sickness for the whole nine months, but at least this time I knew what to expect. The first time round, there had been some days when I had wondered if I was ever going to feel normal again, and psychologically that was hard, but this time it was easier, because I knew it would pass eventually. Aside from feeling nauseous all day, every day, I loved being pregnant. It felt so empowering, and every time I felt him move and kick out his little arms and legs, a wave of sheer happiness would spread across me. It's such a magical feeling. As we had with Charley, we wanted to find out the sex ahead of the birth. When we discovered that we were expecting another boy, we were both over the moon.

Beau was delivered by a good friend of Dr Silverstone. When I set eyes on my new baby for the first time, I fell in love all over again. I felt sure my heart must have expanded. Because Beau was our second child, I felt more grown-up and confident in my ability to be a good mum. With Chaz, I had worried that I wasn't quite ready because of my career and my fertility issues, whereas with Beau, it wasn't such a transition.

Jamie brought Charley to the hospital to meet Beau. To be honest, he was more excited about the present he was going to be given by his baby brother than he was about Beau himself. For the first few days, Charley was quite intrigued by Beau, but then it wore off – newborn babies are just not very entertaining to small children!

Charley and Beau are typical boys. They have always had bags of energy, constantly running around, and they are famous with our friends and family for their never-ending stamina. Charley was always raring to go at one hundred miles an hour, and when Beau arrived, he had to fit in with Charley rather than the other way round. Even when Beau was tiny, I remember taking Charley to a nearby farm in an attempt to wear him out so he would sleep (he never did). Poor Beau was dragged around in the baby carrier with his little legs dangling, while I legged it after Charley.

When Charley was about eight and Beau was four, I took them to Disneyland Paris. We went with two of my friends, who each have four boys. We had the most full-on few days imaginable, going on rides, walking for miles to make sure we saw everything, getting a table for sixteen with everyone's kids at every meal: it was complete chaos. We caught the train home, but there were horrendous delays en route and we were stuck in tunnels for hours, with everyone slowly going increasingly crazy. We'd arranged to be picked up from St Pancras in a minibus, because we all live in the same area. Finally, we arrived, and got off the train and on to the minibus, piling in with our six hundred bags. It was about two o'clock in the morning by this stage, and we were all absolutely whacked. As we pulled up at my friend Carly's house, Charley said: 'Mum, when we get in, can I go on the trampoline?'

The whole bus fell about laughing. That just about sums him up. Even now, my house can be tidy, and then within twenty minutes of Charley getting home, it will be carnage.

Both my boys were the kind of kids that you could not let out of your sight. If you took your eyes off them for a second to look at something or speak to someone, they could be gone. I am also a paranoid mum. Charley was young at around the time of Madeleine McCann's disappearance in Portugal, and what you read and hear can make you so distrustful. Added to this, I'd had an experience when I was about seven that had always stayed with me. We were in Spain on holiday. I was playing in a playground on my own, and my mum, Nana, and Grandad Malcolm were eating dinner nearby. A man drove up to me in his car and, rolling down the window, asked me if I wanted to see some kittens. He told me to get in the back. I knew that something wasn't quite right, so I said no and ran away as fast as I could in my flip-flops back to my family. When I told them what had happened, Grandad Malcolm, who was a big man with arms full of tattoos, hoisted me on to his hip and walked me around to try and find the man, but he was long gone. However irrational it sounds, I've always been nervous about my own children ever having a similar experience.

One of my favourite places to take the kids when they

were small were soft-play centres, because I knew they could run around as much as they wanted, but I'd still be able to keep an eye on them. I would be chatting for a few minutes, and Beau would disappear out of sight. I used to do what my friend Carly called the 'Beau run', where I would sprint like a woman possessed, almost pushing people out of the way, until I could see him – then I could relax. I would be on the verge of heart failure in the time it took to find him. He would always be in a corner somewhere under loads of plastic balls. Once I had laid eyes on him, I could get back to my cup of tea and everything would be fine until about twenty minutes later, when we would go through the whole thing again.

Some of my most special memories are the simplest ones: just sitting at home with my boys, spending time with them and chilling out around the house. When Beau was a baby, I had a routine where I would have Beau in the carrycot and make Charley a little bed on the sofa where he could fall asleep. I would watch *I'm a Celebrity . . . Get Me Out of Here!*, and when the credits rolled, that would be my cue to feed Beau and carry both boys up to bed. As lovely as the holidays and other celebrations were, it is those real moments where we were together and safe that I cherish most. There were no worries or pressures or fires to put out; it was just the four of us.

The boys both really love their sports. I have always been happy looking on from the sidelines, and it was great watching them first get into sport when they were small. When Charley started playing cricket aged about seven or eight, though, I had no idea what I was going to watch. It's the kind of sport where there are loads of fielding positions, and Charley was miles away from the action. About two and a half hours in, he still hadn't been anywhere near the ball. When the ball finally did come towards him, he was busy digging up leaves and conkers! He did actually get much better at cricket as he got older because he was a great batsman, it just took him a little while to cotton on.

Charley is now an amazing rugby player – he's really tall and solid. I hadn't watched much rugby before so it was quite new to me at first, but it's great. He's so big that I don't get nervous, as it's rare that an opponent is bigger than him. Charley can pretty much tackle anybody. I did get told off once, for shouting, 'Take him down!' during a match at school. Another parent told me it wasn't appropriate to encourage my child to take out another kid. Noted!

Beau is into football. He is super-talented, but I know it's going to be tough for him. I worry that whenever Beau or Charley walk on to any sports pitch, whether football or rugby (although perhaps more so with football), they are automatically judged because they are Jamie's sons. Before Beau even starts a game, there is a certain expectation. My heart skips a beat when I hear people talking at one of his matches. It won't be just one of the kids missing a penalty, it will be *a Redknapp kid* missing a penalty, and that makes it a bigger deal. Aside from that, though, I love going to watch him play. Beau has been playing in the under-12s for Chelsea for a few years, and it's such a supportive and non-competitive environment. We've been lucky with the group of parents that we've met, because it feels like we've formed a real community.

Christmas has always been a huge deal in our house – even bigger than all of the birthday celebrations. Over the years, we've established so many traditions. We've always hung stockings in the lounge, but as soon as they were old enough, we would also hang a new pair of football boots over the door handles, so they would be the first thing the boys would see when they came downstairs. It was their sign that Father Christmas had been.

Both of our families would come together, and it was so special to have everyone in one place. Some years we would host, and other years we'd go to Jamie's parents' house. Sometimes we would end up with three enormous tables stretching down the hallways just to fit everyone in. I'm not the best cook in the world, so either my mum or Jamie's mum would be in charge of the cooking, while I was tasked with laying the table. It was always such a magical day.

x x x

Although I took a step back from my own career when the boys were younger, I never got too involved in the world of football. I felt like I needed to stay away from it all, because at some point down the line, I knew I wanted to be in music again. Even so, it still eventually got to a stage where I was known more for being Jamie Redknapp's wife than for being Louise the musician.

Over the years, I met loads of footballers and their wives. I adore many of them, and some of my closest friends were wives of other footballers. (Of course, I met loads of dickheads, too, just as you do in any walk of life.) When you're married to a sportsman, you spend a lot of time on your own because they're away so much, so my friendships with the other wives and partners were important, as we understood and sympathised with each other. I never had a problem with Jamie going off to training camps or being away for work: I knew how driven he was, and respected that because we shared the same mentality when it came to our careers. But it did mean that I was on my own a lot.

One thing that I've always hated about the world of football is the term 'WAG' – it's so derogatory. The word was coined by the press and used mostly in 2006 when England was playing the World Cup in Germany. It comes with horrible connotations and is never used in a nice way. What really bothers me about it is, well, what were those women supposed to do? Were they not allowed to go out together? Were they not supposed to show up and support their partners? If you love some-one, you're always so proud of their achievements and want to be there for them every step of the way. But that doesn't mean you should be reduced to the term 'WAG' – you're still your own person, with your own goals and dreams.

When people throw around phrases like 'WAG', they're not thinking about the kinds of challenges the partners and families of footballers might face. There is so much more to being in a relationship with a footballer than going out and looking a certain way. Of course, being in football offers amazing opportunities, and footballers are paid huge sums of money, but it's not all straightforward. You might be asked to pack up your kids and move countries with forty-eight hours' notice because your husband has been signed to a new team. It's not easy for your kids to be uprooted and to have to leave their friends and schools when they're happy and settled. And what about when it's all over? You might spend months or years supporting your partner after a bad injury, or trying to be there for someone whose career was over at thirty-five and who is now struggling to find a new role because they can never recapture the buzz that they used to feel when they were playing. I know footballers get huge salaries and are massively privileged, but no amount of money can stop life from being challenging and difficult at times.

I know women who not only hold their families together through such challenges, but who have also created their own businesses, speak five languages, and are hugely accomplished and successful in their own right. They are so much more than 'WAGs' – they are intelligent, strong and independent.

x x x

Maybe I haven't always done things exactly right, but I am so proud of the way my boys are growing up. Charley has had to take on a different role since Jamie and I split up. He can be quite fatherly towards Beau, while to me, he is a great friend and ally, as well as my son. Sometimes I'll ask his advice when I am unsure about something. I know he has my back, and we are very similar, so I understand the way he thinks. We both have huge hearts and can be emotional. I know it's tough for anybody whose parents split up, but it's even tougher when you have to read about it in the papers. There was a time when I wondered if they would ever forgive me, but thankfully we have an amazing relationship. Watching them grow up and become teenagers has been such a privilege.

Of the two of them, Beau is much more into music. If either of them grows up to be well known, whether in football or entertainment, I think it will be Beau. He enjoys the showmanship and he has the most fantastic sense of humour. Regardless of the way you parent, I think there are certain feelings that all mums share. One of my favourite moments of the day is school pick-up, when you are looking for each other at the gate and you catch eyes with your child and they walk towards you.

I'm enjoying still being able to have that moment with Beau on most days.

I am particularly proud of how kind my boys are. One thing I always teach my kids, and which my mum taught me, is that kindness is key. I've always said to them that I don't care if their grades are not great as long as they treat other people well. I'd rather they failed every exam than get sent home for bullying or being unkind at school. It is the most important lesson to learn in life. If there are three people interviewing for a job who all have the same abilities, skills and grades, ultimately, the person that will be picked is the one that the interviewers remember for being a great person with good energy. It's something that I feel is central to my own success. There are lots of people who can sing and dance, but being someone who others actually want to be around is what makes a real difference.

You've Got This . . .

Be yourself

I can't remember where I first heard the saying, 'Be yourself. There is nobody better qualified' but I love it and I think it really applies to motherhood. I may not be the perfect mum but I am so, so proud of my kids and I would go to the ends of the earth for them.

Some of the most important lessons I try to teach my kids are to work hard, be fearless and ambitious, and be kind

I don't want them to grow up feeling entitled. I tell them that if we walk into a building and someone opens the door for them, they should always say thank you: firstly, because you never know if that person is going to end up running the company one day; and secondly – and more importantly – because everyone deserves that grace. I want them to be humble: it's something I really believe in.

When I say I encourage them to be ambitious, I don't mean I need them to get the best possible grades or have their whole career path mapped out. Some people are destined for massive careers and others find meaning in different ways – either way, I know they will work out where they want to be. As long as they are kind and respectful, have ambition at something, and are fearless about it, I feel like I have done a good job as a parent.

How to be a good mum in the age of social media

Sometimes I wonder if this is even possible! It's hard to be confident about your parenting when we are all subject to online scrutiny. Everyone will always have an opinion. If I post a picture on social media of myself on a night out, I'll be bombarded with accusatory questions about why I'm not with Charley and Beau instead. 'Not with your boys?' people will type. In reality, I'm probably in the middle of making them spaghetti Bolognese, having just posted a picture from four nights before. But I shouldn't have to explain to anybody that I spend most of my time with my kids. Social media is a snapshot of someone else's life, it cannot and will not ever paint the whole picture. It is easy to see things out of context online. It's like reading a sentence of a book without finishing the chapter.

When I split up with Jamie, the accusations came in thick and fast. I was so heavily judged, and it amazed me that so many people, including other women, made assumptions about what I was or wasn't doing when it came to my kids. I noticed real double standards: women are simply expected to be with their kids, whereas if fathers spend any time with their children, then suddenly they are 'Super Dad' or Dad of the Year. They are described as 'babysitting' rather than simply spending time with their own children. As soon as fathers play an active role, they are seen as heroes. Why is it that men are praised for the very things women do every day? This is not a criticism of Jamie, who is a fantastic dad, but of society's perception of parenthood as a whole. This has to change, as women cannot be it all and have it all. Every parent plays an important role in the upbringing of their kids; we should all be equal in this equation. Now that I'm on my own, I feel this is even more magnified. At times, I feel like I am constantly having to defend my choice to work. But the fact now is that not only do I want to work, I also *need* to work.

I am not going to play the social media game of putting my kids on Instagram just to show the world they are with me. The day I have to prove to society that I'm a good mum is the day it's really gone wrong for me. My boys know, and I know, and that's all that matters. But I'm not going to lie: when my self-esteem has been low, some comments have really stung me, especially when they have been untrue.

However you choose to parent is the right way for you and your family

When children are babies, everyone has their own idea about the right way to do stuff. Whether you choose to breastfeed or not, co-sleep or not, go to work or stay at home, being a parent means you are automatically judged in some way. For new mums especially, I think self-doubt is a completely normal emotion, but it's important to remember that every new parent is simply trying to do their best. I think people who criticise others are often trying to cover up their own insecurities or guilt about things they feel they should've done differently. Equally, it can be easy to look at other people's choices and question them, especially if they are different to your own, but everyone's situation is unique to them. Sometimes, what comes across as judgement is simply ignorance, because people don't know the whole story. For example, when I had my Caesareans, it was because that was the safest option for me; it wasn't because I didn't want to give birth naturally. As mothers, we know our children better than anyone. Be confident in what you believe is best for you and your kids. What others think simply does not matter.

It is important to take time out for yourself

So many women I know – myself included – are guilty of not making themselves a priority. It's as if when we become mothers, we give up all our individuality and we have to shift to being someone who is completely selfless. Yes, being a mother may be the most important job there is, but it is not all that defines you.

I often struggle with feelings of guilt if I go anywhere or do anything that's just for me. Men never worry when they take a day out for themselves, so why is it that women feel guilty for it? Even going to work can feel like a guilt trip sometimes. Let's be honest: we all judge women who are out all the time, so it's clear what's needed here is a total shift in mindset. How can we keep going if we never take a break to enjoy the things that we love? Doing that should never make us feel bad. What is better for your kids: to have your full and undivided focus twenty-four hours a day, leaving you feeling exhausted, down and frustrated, or to sometimes have you for a little less time, but as the best version of a mum you can be? When I'm with my kids, I want to be happy and owning my parenting skills. So whether it's going to the gym, spending time with friends or enjoying a hobby, it's really important to take time for yourself.

It can be particularly tough being a single parent

When you are raising kids in a relationship, you and your partner have the freedom to swap the 'goodie' and 'baddie' roles, but when you're a single parent, even if you are co-parenting, you always want to be the 'good' parent and the person your kids love being with. I don't want to be the cross one. I am quite soft and sometimes too easy-going. When I tell my boys off or we have a disagreement, I often panic afterwards as I may not be with them the next day. I know discipline is important because it will stand them in good stead for the future, but it can feel like a challenge – so some days, they probably get away with more than they should!

I'm not perfect by any stretch of the imagination, and do worry that I'm not strict enough. But my kids are kids, and I do my best. It is so important to me that my home should be a safe space for my boys. For me, the outside world is not somewhere I can let my guard down, so it's vital that my home feels like a happy and safe place.

One of the things that really affects me as a mother is 'mum guilt' or 'mum-shaming'

If I'm out for a couple of drinks with my girlfriends, I find myself constantly worrying that I've been out too long, that I'm having too much fun, and that I might be judged for it. If I go on holiday with some of my girlfriends, or even just out for a meal in the evening and I'm photographed, it feels like I'm suddenly being seen as a terrible mother. I find it crazy how people can completely ignore everything that I do for my kids and make a snap judgement about my parenting skills based on a random photo or news story, but I know this isn't something unique to me. Whether you are in the public eye or not, all parents feel that pressure to live up to an impossibly high standard.

I've also experienced that sense of 'mum guilt' or 'mum-shaming'. I am not the type of mum who reads all the emails from school and is ready with the money, gifts or costumes needed for every event. Having a school-age child is like a job in itself! There have been times when I have felt really uncomfortable at the school gates, as though some of the other mums are looking down on me or judging me. I have always tried to be at pick-up unless I am working, but I have never lingered for the car-park chats and I am not interested in gossiping about which child has done what, or who has won something or is going off to a certain school. That is just not me. For some time after I split with Jamie, I found the school run particularly stressful. Not only were the paparazzi often following me, but I felt like all the 'clipboard mums' were looking at me and judging me for my choices. For some time, my own mum picked up the boys for me because I just couldn't face it.

Our kids definitely teach us, too!

Motherhood does change you: in a way, I think we grow up with our children. My kids have taught me so much, and I'm still learning from them all the time. I love the way they never hold grudges and just accept each other. One day I was talking with Beau about a pretty girl in his class. When I asked him if she was his girlfriend, he told me that no, she was his friend Sam's girlfriend and he was second choice – so if it went wrong, he was next in line. I asked him if he minded. No, he said, he was happy for Sam and happy with the set-up. Kids can be so funny and have none of the hang-ups that adults can have. They don't linger over petty rows and seem to be able to reset every day and just get on with it.

Not that long ago, I was sitting with Charley after a bad day and he told me to stop thinking negative thoughts, as they were just upsetting me and nobody else. He told me that I needed to focus on the positive things that were going on and just switch my mindset. How right he was! I love the way that kids are so spontaneous and have that capacity to seek out fun regardless of what day of the week it is. They remind us that the best moments in life are unplanned. They know who they are and are unapologetic about it.

Chapter Five

LEARN TO ACCEPT AND LOVE YOUR BODY

'There is nothing more rare, nor more beautiful, than a woman being unapologetically herself; comfortable in her perfect imperfection. To me, that is the true essence of beauty.'

Steve Maraboli, *Unapologetically You*

'Hey, Mum!'

As I looked over, Beau ran up and splashed me before diving back into the sea. I squealed with laughter as I wiped the water from my face.

It was a beautiful, picture-postcard morning in Barbados and I was messing around in the clear blue water with Jamie, Beau and Charley. Some days, I would get nervous that there would be photographers around and I'd ask Jamie to take the boys to the beach by himself. But as we'd looked out from the hotel that morning, the coast was close to empty, with just a few other people milling about and setting themselves up for the day. It was the perfect opportunity to enjoy some time at the beach.

It had become a bit of a tradition for our family to go to Barbados every January for some winter sun. We stayed in amazing hotels, and with that came a certain amount of privacy, but the reality was that we were often targets for the 'paps' – or paparazzi.

That day, the boys were in their element, swimming, messing about and laughing. But one second we were all having fun, and the next thing I knew there was something odd going on. Three guys with rucksacks came jogging on to the beach, just a few minutes apart. One went and stood brazenly to the side of us, another ducked behind a kayak, while the third guy pitched up on a sunbed and stuck a towel over his head, with his black long camera lens sticking out from underneath. It was a pretty rubbish attempt at flying under the radar – they couldn't have looked more conspicuous on a mostly empty family beach if they tried.

It was a moment of sheer panic. My stomach turned, a feeling of nausea rose in my throat and paranoia swept over me. My heart started hammering. Suddenly, I was no longer enjoying myself. I felt trapped and anxious. I couldn't stay in the water forever, but I knew as soon I headed back to my sunbed they would start snapping away.

Beaches, bikinis and the potential for bad angles are just the worst. That was at the start of our holiday, so I wasn't even armed with a tan! Although I knew rationally that I had a nice enough figure, and that I was on an incredible holiday on a beautiful beach, there was just a small part of me that felt absolutely terrified about what the pictures would look like. I was also too embarrassed to even admit that to anyone, as I didn't want to sound like I was self-obsessed. But sometimes you just can't help how you feel inside.

I know that how I see myself is not how others see me. I think there is a certain ideal body image for women – one that many of us subscribe to – that simply isn't realistic. I'm my own harshest critic, but all it takes is for the camera to catch a bad angle – maybe as you're bending down to pick something up or lying a bit strangely on a sunbed – and it completely distorts the shape of your body so that you end up looking horrendous. I knew this, logically, but I also knew that the photos would still upset me.

'Jamie, I can't believe this. They're taking photos of us!' I said, feeling increasingly fretful.

'Don't worry about it,' he told me. 'You're fine. Forget it.'

It's all right for you, I thought. *You look great.*

Jamie was all six-pack and toned shoulders – and besides, men are never judged and analysed in the same way that women are. That's just how it is. For every hundred articles commenting on a woman's figure, there are only ever one or two – if that – that focus on men.

I know it might sound a bit dramatic, but after that

day, I didn't go back to the beach for the rest of the holiday. Even when we were sitting around the hotel pool, I would have my towel clutched around me until the final second before I jumped into the water. When I was by the pool, I put my dress on while I was lying down, contorting myself into strange shapes to do so; who knows what the other people around the pool thought I was doing.

A couple of days later, I got a text from a friend: 'Hey, Lou, just seen the pics of you and Jamie online. It looks like you are having a great time! See you soon! X'

Those same anxious feelings returned as I searched for the images online. It felt horrible. Even writing this down makes me feel a bit ridiculous, but it was how I felt. It was as if my body was on show for the whole world to look at and pull apart.

The friend who had texted me would have had no idea that the photos would be so upsetting. Unless something is written or said directly about you, it is often hard to understand what effect it will have. She probably just thought they looked like photos of us enjoying a lovely family holiday.

I tried to ignore the press and just live in the moment, but it was hard not to worry. I couldn't shake the feeling that there might be a pap lurking nearby, ready to jump out and snap a photo. Now I look back and wonder why I cared so much, but at the time, I just felt so exposed.

x x x

Body image, weight, curves ... these are things that so many women struggle with, and I am no exception. Negative body image has at times taken a significant toll on my mental and physical health. Like many other women, there have been times in my life when I have been consumed with the idea of having the 'perfect body'. Even when I was a size eight in my teens and early twenties, I felt like I was half a stone too heavy, that my stomach should be flatter, or that my body could be a slightly different shape. The quest for this flawless and slimline 'perfect' body has taken up so much time and energy over the years and I am still working hard at accepting and loving myself as I am.

People say that stage schools can be an environment where body hang-ups start to take hold, but this wasn't the case for me. When I was at school, there wasn't a huge amount of emphasis on our weight. We were all dancers, so we were aware of our shapes and changing teenage figures, but it was never a big issue. It wasn't really spoken about and none of us were self-conscious. However, I was beginning to see that it wasn't just talent you needed; for some roles, you needed to be a certain shape or build. When we were all fifteen or sixteen, there was a stage where some people were developing and getting boobs and a bum, while others were less developed, but it never felt like a big issue.

During my Eternal days and when I was singing on my own, I was always in the studio and dancing all the time. My job kept me busy and on my feet, and my adrenaline was always running high. At first, I never questioned pictures of myself. This was before digital photography, so all the pictures were taken using negatives and they were much more natural, like the shot Mario Sorrenti took of me for 'Light of My Life'.

Things changed when pictures became digital, as they were routinely touched up to look better. Of course, all images have some sort of lighting that makes them look a certain way, and this has always been the case, but as time went on, I found that the digital manipulation of my pictures was increasing – not necessarily to make me look skinnier, but to give a glossier and more polished finish, with smooth, bright skin and a 'perfect' look. I often remind myself that to look like this in real life without technology is completely unachievable.

Throughout my career, the way I look has always played such a key role in how I am seen and presented. At times, I feel like how I look has been rammed down my throat for over twenty years. The truth is, I hate seeing pictures of myself. That might be hard to comprehend because I have been photographed so much over so many years. Having my picture taken is one of the things I know how to do, and it is part and parcel of my job, but that doesn't mean that I always love the pictures. Far from it. I scrutinise every detail and pick my images apart.

After I had Charley, my life became less about work and was more focused around family life. With this shift, pictures of me went from being images from professional photoshoots to hastily snapped pap shots. Before then, I'd been used to seeing pictures of myself without a hair out of place. When pictures are chosen for magazine interviews or music promotion, the images go through many rounds of edits and are always signed off by various people, so seeing these unedited shots of myself in my bikini or just snapped when I was out and about was always a shock. I found it almost impossible not to compare myself to other women.

Many people in the public eye 'set up' pictures of themselves. This means they tell the paps they are going to be somewhere and effectively pose for them. The pictures are staged, but made to look like casual shots of them doing things like walking the dog or lying on the beach. Sometimes, the celebrities even take a cut of the proceeds as payment for tipping off the photographers. I've been offered this deal countless times, but I would never go for it. Everyone's different and I will never judge anyone else's decision to go down this route, but any pictures out there of me in a bikini on holiday or out with my friends are the result of paps hiding somewhere and taking the photos without my knowledge. I know it comes with the territory, but it has always given me such bad anxiety: whenever there are paps around, I panic. It means I can never truly relax in a public space, and that is not easy.

People always tell me that the pictures will be gone tomorrow and that no one cares. I know they're probably right but it doesn't change how I feel. When friends text me to tell me I'm in the paper with my boob out, they expect me to say, 'God, really?' and shrug it off, but the feelings I go through are more visceral. I examine every inch of myself. Some days, there are great pictures, and there is something very empowering about seeing a picture of yourself in the newspaper that has been taken by a skilful photographer who has chosen the angle and lighting beautifully – it can make you feel like a million dollars and leave you with a spring in your step. The counterbalance, though, is those pictures where you have been shot from a distance with your leg in a weird position, with overhead lighting shadowing your whole body and an odd expression on your face. These images make you want to hide away from the world.

I've always been aware that my relationship with the press was a two-way thing. Early on in my career, someone I trusted told me that if you don't call the press looking for publicity, when it's a quiet news day they will respect you and leave you alone. Yes, I will do interviews and have my picture taken for work, but I don't court unnecessary publicity: it's just not me. I try to be as upfront and honest as I can, but there are times in life when you deserve a certain level of privacy. And I think I will always find having my photo taken without my permission a horrible experience.

There have been times in my life when my relationship with food and my own body image has become particularly unhealthy. In 2007, I was asked to take part in the documentary *The Truth About Size Zero*. Charley was a toddler then, and it was the first big job I'd been asked to do since having him. The premise was that I would go on a military-style fitness drive to drop from a size eight to a size four, which is the equivalent of US size zero. I was really slight back then anyway, but knew that girls my size would still not get certain jobs because they needed to be even skinnier, although no one would ever say this in as many words. At the time, the size zero phenomenon was a big deal. It was felt that even a size eight wasn't slim enough, and it seemed that the goal-posts were just constantly shifting, pushing us towards increasingly unrealistic 'ideals'.

Before we started, the programme-makers sent me to see a doctor. The doctor told me that according to my BMI, I was underweight, so they felt it wasn't healthy for me to do the show. Despite the people around me gently suggesting that it might be a bad idea, I was determined that I wanted to do it and I dug my heels in. Secretly, I had always wanted to be skinnier, and I knew I could do the programme justice. In the end, I agreed to put weight on before the show started, and I gained about half a stone before we started filming. I started the diet at 7 stones 10lbs. A photographer took a photo of me in workout clothes, standing in a neutral pose with my hands on my hips. It was not touched up, and I was shocked by my appearance; I thought I looked really overweight. If I had been pictured in a magazine like that, I would've been mortified. Looking back now, I can see that I was perfectly healthy.

There were doctors and nutritionists monitoring my weight and health, and the doctor in charge laid out the risks to the extreme diet. He told me that it could harm every system in my body; that my fertility could be affected; that I would be put at increased risk of getting an infection; that I might get sleep disturbances; and that my muscles could break down, including those around my heart. He said he hoped that I would not do it. While I was pretty shocked by what he had to say, I still wanted to go ahead with the show.

I flew over to LA to start the diet and workout regime with Barry Jay from Barry's Bootcamps. On the plane over, I ate so many bread rolls, knowing they would be my last proper food for a while. No one was very happy about me going. My mum was really worried that I would go on the diet and like it, and would then stay that way. Although Jamie thought I was mad and was concerned I would lose my boobs and my bum, he was also supportive because he knew I really wanted to take part in the show.

The show started with me meeting a celebrity stylist. Together, we bought a size-zero dress that I would hang in my wardrobe. My aim would be to fit into it at the end of the programme. It was tiny, like something a pre-teen girl would wear.

I was told not to eat anything bigger than the size of my fist for each meal. I was to eat oats and omelettes for breakfast, and fish or vegetables for lunch and supper. I wasn't allowed any dairy or much colour in my diet – even fruit was off the menu. I was resolute, determined that I was going to do it properly because the programme would not work otherwise. It needed to be real, and I wanted the show to be a success. I was only allowed to eat 500 calories a day and my workouts needed to burn off 1,000 calories. This deficit of 500 calories a day would mean I could lose a stone within four weeks. I spent a lot of time working out, doing a three-mile run followed by an hour of weights. I hate exercising because I find it so boring, and I found that one of the hardest aspects of the diet.

I also hated the intrusion of having the cameras around me all the time. Until then, my work had involved turning up, getting my hair and make-up done, giving an interview and performing, and then leaving. All of a sudden, there were cameras on me all the time and people around me, asking constant questions.

At the time, I was also doing some presenting on *The Clothes Show*, and I chatted with the models about the pressure to stay thin. Being a size zero was the aim for a lot of people in the public eye. There has always been real pressure to look a certain way, and we'd been made to believe that the skinnier you were, the better the clothes would look. I love editorial fashion, so I am not that girl who wants to wear a Hérve Léger dress and look sexy; I want to wear a white T-shirt with no bra, some Levi's hanging off my hips and a nice heel. I love the androgynous look, but I am five foot four with natural curves, so I'm not really built like that. Many of the models and people I talked to had the same struggles. I can imagine that a lot of fashion houses and designers care about their clothes looking good on the catwalk, and believe they look better on someone taller and skinnier.

For the first ten days, I found the plan really hard to follow. I was hungry all the time and really irritable and tired. But I knew how much money and time had been invested, so I needed to stick to it. On days that I was working, I had to work out first thing in the morning and last thing at night, and it became quite mind-numbing.

After those first ten days, though, I found that I was quickly falling into a pattern of not wanting to eat and trying to exert complete control over my diet. Even when I ate the small amount that I was allowed on the plan, I started to feel guilty. It became startlingly clear to me how easy it would be to slip into a mindset of obsessively counting calories and weighing yourself all the time. All of a sudden, it felt real. I'd gone from making a TV programme for work to actually nervously monitoring my calorie intake.

As part of the show, I visited a unit dedicated to treating children with eating disorders. I found it heartbreaking to hear their stories. They were at what should have been the most carefree time of their lives, talking about not wanting to drink water because it might make them put on weight. This upset me so much – but even then, I couldn't quite make the connection between the way their minds were working and the direction that I was heading in.

The same was true for the section in the programme that I shot with my friend, Sophie. The cameras filmed us talking about her experience with anorexia. Sophie and I had been great friends at school. We spent a lot of time with each other's families and would go to each other's homes after school and on weekends. Both our families were the type who would always do a dessert, so the main course would be followed by an apple pie, Arctic roll, or crumble and custard. Food was never an issue. Our friendship continued when we left Conti's, and while I went off to work with Eternal, Sophie went into the modelling world. When I finished in the studio, I would go and see her, and when she had completed a job, she would come over and see me. She went to Japan to do some modelling when we were about twenty, and I remember meeting up with her one day when she came home. I only needed to look at her to realise that she was seriously unwell. She had gone beyond skinny. Her leggings looked like trousers on her; they literally just hung from her legs. Her arms and cheeks were gaunt and she looked quite grey. Shortly afterwards, she was hospitalised and was told she had just four days to live. I didn't know what turned it around for her, but thankfully she made a remarkable recovery.

When I was asked to do the programme, I felt having that experience of being by Sophie's side would help me, but weirdly it didn't seem to sort my head out. Even seeing and talking to Sophie during filming didn't make me question how I was starting to feel. I knew what I was doing was unhealthy, but the feeling of power I had over my body when I wasn't eating was somehow intoxicating. Suddenly, I could see how she and those girls at the clinic had got to that point. My energy levels had completely dropped, and I was getting moody, often snapping at Jamie and Charley. At one point, when Jamie and I had a small row about something, he told me in a playful way to, 'Get your scrawny neck out of here.' And in that moment, it felt like a *compliment*. I mean, who thinks being told they're scrawny is a *good* thing? But I was so happy about it.

After about three weeks, the doctor told me to stop, but even then I wouldn't listen to him. By that point, I found solace in the gym, and would hang the dress above the treadmill to give myself extra motivation. I *had* to fit into it. I headed back to LA for a few days, and I was happy to be away from home, with all its comforts and temptations. Barry was telling me that I looked great and how exciting it all was, and I believed him. I had my picture taken by the same photographer who'd taken the workout clothes shot at the beginning of the project. I thought I looked fantastic. The longer I had spent feeling hungry, the more I had become used to that feeling. Now, the idea of feeling full seemed scary to me. But the dress fitted. The narrative of the show was me then throwing that impossibly tiny dress into the bin and going out with my friends for dinner, but honestly?

I adored that dress and how I looked in it. It was how I had always wanted to look.

When I walked through the door at home after the experiment, I remember my mum looking at Jamie in a slightly horrified way. I thought I looked great, but my mum tells me that all she wanted to do was spend the next weeks and months fattening me up.

The doctor was quite stern about the danger I had put my body through. My BMI was now in the range that would indicate a diagnosis of anorexia and my oestrogen levels had dropped. I'd also lost five pounds of muscle. This meant I ran the risk of putting on more weight afterwards, which could lead to yo-yo dieting.

There was very good aftercare following the show, and it was written into my contract with the show that I would regain the weight I had lost. I was told that I needed to introduce one new thing each day into my diet. I also knew that I could not eat normally, as I was at risk of putting on more weight than I had lost. My favourite food then was a tuna bagel, so I started to order one every day from a little café in South Molton Street in London that served the best food. I would sit outside with my bagel and a cup of tea. Within two weeks, I started to put the weight back on, and I think I got back to a healthier weight through just eating that one thing.

Despite all the health risks and the emotional strain of being so skinny, I was still torn about putting weight back on. It was like I was becoming everything that I had seen around me while filming, and I was getting into the mindset of the women that I had interviewed in hospital. For a time, I could see how easy it would be to slip into having an eating disorder. The fact I now knew I could control my eating in that way made it even harder. It took me a long time to get over it, and it was a gradual process. I knew I had to get back to normal. We went out for dinner with friends a lot, or had them over for meals, and it was impossible for me not to eat. I didn't want it to become a talking point that I wasn't eating in the same way I had before doing the programme, so I just started eating like I always had before. I did resist it initially, but it was inevitable that unless I avoided meals with other people, I would need to start eating again – and I did.

As time went on, my weight moved back to where it sits comfortably, but there have still been times when I've found myself fighting against it. It seemed like the pressure on all of us to look good was increasing. After Charley, I didn't notice much pressure to ping back to my pre-pregnancy shape, but by the time Beau arrived five years later, it felt like there was this expectation that I should be back in my size-eight jeans within just a few weeks. It seemed to be more of a 'thing'. The pressure to look a certain way has been a source of constant stress for such a long time, and I know that being in the public eye has only made this worse.

You've Got This ...

There's undoubtedly huge pressure on women to look a certain way

I can't count the number of times I've taken a photo of myself and then deleted it because I don't like how my body looks. There is an expectation that women should conform to a certain size or shape, but it's completely unrealistic – we're all built differently, and that's what makes us unique. Some people are naturally very slim. My mum, for example, is really tiny and she always eats what she wants – she wouldn't think twice about having a doughnut. She is very healthy, but she never deprives herself of a meal or something sweet. I always wanted to be slim but that pressure never came from my family, who always had a normal, healthy attitude to food.

Learn to accept what you have – and work with it

Am I happy with everything about myself? No. Would I like a fat-free body with no wobbles? Yes. But I have learned to accept my body the way it is it, and I know it's never really going to change very much. Being happy with your body does not mean that you have to think it's perfect; it simply means embracing the imperfections. You can lose loads of weight, but I think your body will almost always naturally go back to where it is comfortable. There have been times where I've lost loads of weight, for example when I have been depressed or when I did *Strictly*, but I've always bounced back to the same sort of size afterwards. While I may not love my body completely, I am learning that it is OK to just be me. I know that being the 'perfect' size is ultimately not what will make me happy, because inner happiness can never equate to what you wear or how much you weigh; it is about feeling comfortable in your own skin. True happiness comes from loving who you really are. Of course, old habits are hard to break. I still have moments of wanting to be different or disliking myself when I eat loads of unhealthy food. It can make me start to panic, but then I have a word with myself.

Finding a form of exercise you love is important

Ultimately, it is all about balance and finding a lifestyle that is both healthy and sustainable in the long term. For me, the tricky part of keeping fit is finding something that I really love and enjoy. I am definitely not a gym bunny, and I tend to dip in and out of trying new things. If you want to stay fit but don't enjoy the gym, then try to find another way of being active that works for you. My job has always kept me fit, and now I love dance as a way of working out. I have found a trainer who understands this, and we move a lot and include dance in my workouts, which works for me. I also enjoy working out with other people. If I am on my own, I drift into my own head too much, which I know is not good for me. Exercise is a known mood-booster and I always try to make fitness fun, because the minute it becomes a chore, I want to run away.

Don't confine yourself to the treadmill – be creative! That documentary aside, I have never been one for fad diets and have always enjoyed lots of fruit, veggies and protein in my meals. Green juice and a run is just not my style – for me, a cup of tea and a biscuit is a much better option.

When perfection becomes an obsession, it is time to seek professional help

There are many different types of issues that people may have with food, many of which are related to body image. It doesn't matter what you look like or how much you weigh – if your relationship with eating and food is affecting your health, you must talk to someone about it. As I've told you, I found myself on the cusp of an eating disorder, and after my own experiences and seeing what my friend Sophie went through, I know that recovery starts with admitting there is a problem and getting help from a doctor, therapist or support group. Thankfully, my mental health issues around food were short-lived, but if you find yourself obsessing over your weight, or are worried about someone close to you, there are many places to turn, including charities like Beat and Mind.

Getting to a place where I love and accept my body is hard, and it is still work in progress

I know that being the 'perfect' size is not the key to confidence, success, or happiness. I know some people worry about other aspects of their appearance, like their skin, height or hair. I have learned to surround myself with people who don't make me feel like I need to lose weight or compete with them to look a certain way. I have learned that I will never be anyone else other than me. If I feel I need to be better or skinnier than the people I am with, it can never be a proper friendship. I know I have to offer people more than how I look or my body. If my personality is not enough for someone, then I know they're not someone I want to spend time with. Surround yourself with people who support you and only want the best for you.

Believe me when I say there are unrealistic images of beauty everywhere

Anyone can look great after a professional makeover, a photo-shoot with great lighting, or just putting their picture through ten filters before posting it on social media. It's important never to compare our real selves to these images – or, indeed, to anyone else. Aspire to look like yourself, not the unrealistic ideals of beauty we see that, most of the time, are not even real. Even if you would like to tone up a bit and lose a few pounds, that won't change the shape of your hips or your bodily proportions. We come in all shapes and sizes, so do yourself a favour and buy the clothes that fit you best, not something three sizes too small – it will only make you miser-able. Now I try to celebrate the parts of my body that I love, and focus on the great stuff my body does for me: I've given birth twice, I can dance, I am healthy. Being sexy isn't about being skinny. Women should have the right to wear whatever they want, and should wear whatever makes them happy. I sometimes think of clothing as an expression of my personality, so if the clothes fit and I love them, why shouldn't I wear them? When you're in the public eye, everyone seems to have an opinion on how you look – or how you could look better. Not long ago, someone posted under one of my pictures, 'If you were slimmer, you'd be nice-looking.' As hard as I try to remember that it doesn't matter what someone I don't know thinks about me, it's still really hard not to dwell on it. I used to be much more worried about what people would think when they saw pictures of me, but now I'm older, I don't think anyone is as harsh a critic as we can sometimes be to ourselves. I never look at a curvier woman on the beach in a bikini and think she doesn't look good. I just see a gorgeous, sexy woman, and wish I had the confidence to carry off what she is wearing.

Two seconds on an app can make you look glossy, glamorous and two dress sizes smaller

These days, it's so easy to use filters and edit images to change how we look. For a long time, picture editors were criticised for doctoring photographs of celebrities because of the unrealistic beauty standards this creates, but the truth of the matter is that now photo-editing apps do this for all of us. Whether we want to admit it or not, social media is definitely affecting our ideas of what it is to be 'normal'. The average woman in the UK is a size sixteen, but how many unedited images of curvy women do you see on Instagram?

I am thankful that body positivity seems to control more of the narrative around body image now, and that our culture is starting to embrace different body types. Stars like Kim Kardashian, Rihanna and Beyoncé have more curvaceous figures that make me feel better about my own curves. But women are still picked apart because of how they look. The newspapers are always full of headlines about certain female stars looking 'svelte', 'sizzling', or 'showing off their phenom-enal figure'. There seems to be a whole vocabulary that's been built for talking about how women look on holiday, from 'washboard abs' to 'flaunting her toned body'. Sometimes, these captions are printed accompanying the kind of less flat-tering images I used to worry about, which I feel then drives the keyboard warriors to start typing cruel comments about how the person in the picture doesn't look as good as the headline claims. And why don't the headlines ever mention the person enjoying themselves or looking happy? Everything always points back to women's physicality. Sometimes people wonder why celebrities become obsessed with their weight, but if you just take five minutes out of your day to read the comments under a photo of a woman in a bikini, it becomes clear. It doesn't matter who you are, what you read about yourself does affect you.

There will always be someone saying this woman is too big and this one is too small; you just can't win. Curate your own social media feeds and unfollow anyone who makes you feel bad or as if you need to look a different way. Only follow people who make you feel empowered and happy.

We are not just our bodies

True body confidence comes from within, and celebrating who you are as a person is part of that. I try to tell myself things I like about myself that are not related to how I look. The fact that I can make people laugh and smile has nothing to do with the size of my jeans. I know it's a cliché, but size really is just a number. We need to stop chasing numbers. Put a value on who you are and why the people closest to you love you. Are you a great person? That's all you need to know. I'm still on this journey myself, but I am learning to see my own value and worth, whatever size I am. The perfect body is one that allows us to live our lives as we wish to.

Chapter Six

NEVER PUT OTHER PEOPLE'S HAPPINESS BEFORE YOUR OWN

'Be happy for this moment; this moment is
your life.'

Omar Khayyam

I stood, frozen, at the top of the steps, looking down
at the other female contestants. Laura Whitmore
and Daisy Lowe were in gorgeous silk dresses with
glitzy sparkles and Latin shoes, looking utterly glamorous – and there I was in a red sailor's outfit with white
jazz shoes. I don't think I'd worn white jazz shoes since
I was about twelve. To top it all off, my hair had been
styled into a side ponytail with a cutesy ribbon. I looked
like one of those dolls you put on the Christmas tree.

How is it that I look like this in week one? I wondered.
I'm almost the oldest contestant here and I look like a dolly!

As the intro music played, I walked down the steps with my dance partner, Kevin Clifton. When we reached the bottom, I froze. 'I can't remember the first step,' I whispered to Kevin. 'What's the first step?' I was panicking.

He sang and mimed the actions.

'OK. And what comes after that?' I asked, my mind completely blank.

'You can't remember any of it?' he said. 'We're just about to do it on national TV!'

'I can't remember it!'

Instead of going to his starting position, he took a moment to run through the first bit of the routine with me to try to get it back into my head. That first week we were doing the jive, an incredibly energetic and demanding dance, and there was a lot of content in this particular routine. As they were calling our names, I genuinely had no idea what the first step was. But when the music started, it all came back to me – and I was off.

I was genuinely terrified. After the show, once I was back in my dressing room, I rang my manager. 'I am not doing that again!' I said. 'Can we say I'm ill or I've broken something? What would I need to break – a toe? A finger?' It sounded like I was joking, but I was being deadly serious.

'Lou, don't be so bloody stupid,' she said. 'You're great at this – you light up on that stage. Look, just give it one more week.'

x x x

I loved being married, and once Charley came along, I fell into the routine of being at home, enjoying my role as a wife and mother. I had recorded an album when I was pregnant with him, but the more time that passed, the harder it became to think about releasing it. I kept thinking, 'Give me six more months, give me a year and then I will be ready.'

Of course, that never happened. And by then, I was out of contract with my record company, so it wasn't like I had a team of people waiting for me to produce music. Financially, I didn't need to work, and Jamie was earning more money than I could have anyway at that stage. I would've given my right arm to get back to performing, but the fear of failure and the thought of being away from my sons stopped me. Not doing it became a much easier option than taking the plunge and trying to get back into music. At the same time, I was seeing people that had been doing really well in the music industry just a few years ago failing, struggling to make a success of newer material. That only served to increase my reluctance to dip my toe back into the industry.

I also had a new management team. My previous management had been music-led, but then I joined an agency that did everything, meaning there was more opportunity for TV and branding deals. My decision to step away from music was a conscious one, but that doesn't mean it was what I truly wanted. I did it because it felt like my options had changed. I always find branding stuff hard, because I've never desperately wanted to be famous. I got into the industry because I loved music – all I wanted to do was to sing my own songs, stand on a West End stage and perform. I was desperate to do the things I love. But I was told that in order to play the lead in a West End show, you had to be someone who would shift tickets, which meant staying in the public eye and maintaining a high profile. Switching management felt like the right thing to do, as it opened so many doors and Jamie and I were offered incredible opportunities. In the beginning, I took the lead on branding deals and made decisions about what we did and didn't do, because at that point I'd been in the entertainment world for a bit longer. We both just wanted to be known for our passions and our work, but we still did bits and pieces of branding work if we felt like the opportunity was right for us as a family.

When it came to partnerships and who we'd work with, I was always adamant that we'd only work with names that we genuinely believed in. You can't pull the wool over the public's eyes when it comes to being authentic. I think it's really obvious when people are doing branding deals just for the cash. This has always been one of my golden rules, and even though I still get a lot offers to work with all sorts of brands, I'll only work with the ones that I really like.

I did bits and pieces of TV and other work, and it felt good to not be reliant on Jamie. I used to say, 'I want to earn enough money every year so you never have to feel like you've kept me.' I said it so often that it felt like a bit of a catchphrase. Even though we shared everything during our marriage – Jamie was honestly the most generous guy you could ever wish to meet – I always wanted to contribute.

One of the things I got into was TV presenting. I co-presented *Something for the Weekend* for two years, alongside Tim Lovejoy and Simon Rimmer. I'd always been a fan of the show and loved watching it. The guys were brilliant, and the presenting side of the job suited me down to the ground, but sometimes I'd be standing there chopping carrots and wondering what on earth I was doing cooking and talking about casseroles on national TV. I was told that doing the show would be good for my profile, especially if I wanted to step into a bigger music or entertainment-based show, as I needed a presence on TV, so I played the game. I'm not ungrateful for the opportunity, and I honestly adored the programme itself (and still do), but I never really felt fulfilled. Let's just say cooking isn't one of my strengths.

There were other shows too. It might seem slightly random, but *Farmer Wants a Wife* for Channel 5 was one of my best TV jobs ever. It was honestly such a laugh and made me realise that I enjoy working with the general public the most. The premise of the show was that in each episode, a farmer tried to find his ideal wife, with some help from me – I was essentially playing Cupid. You could never meet anyone more unassuming than a bunch of farmers in the countryside. No one had an agenda, and the participants were genuinely just there to find love. We all stayed in caravans on the sites where we were filming. Once we were staying on a pig farm, and the pigs really screamed – it was terrifying. I felt like I was on the set for *Silence of the Lambs*! I'm a real animal lover, so didn't enjoy seeing the pigs being taken off to slaughter; that was a bit much. But *Farmer Wants a Wife* was a lovely, gentle programme, and it was so nice to properly connect with the people on the show and find out about their lives, their likes and their dislikes.

My absolute TV highlight, though, was judging *So You Think You Can Dance?* on BBC One, alongside Nigel Lythgoe, Arlene Phillips and Sisco Gomez. It felt like all my other TV work had been a stepping stone towards this. I started off as a guest judge and was then invited back. The show tied in with my passion for dance, and I think I sat well in that space between being a performer and a normal member of the public. Thanks to my background, I'd been through similar training to the contestants on the show, so I knew how they felt. I've also been lucky enough to work with some of the best choreographers in the world, which really helped me with knowing what to look out for when I was watching the dancers. When it came to the judging, it was important to be honest. I would never just tell anyone they were crap, but I also wouldn't lie to someone's face. My aim was to give useful advice on how the dancers could improve – plus I felt like I had something to offer as a performer. Seeing the routines the contestants created each week was such a thrill. When all is said and done, I absolutely love dancing and always have, so the fact I was being paid to watch people dance was such a privilege. Doing the show was great fun, and I'd love to do it again or work on something similar in a judging capacity now that I'm older, more confident and less worried about what people think.

As well as presenting, I also got more involved in acting. I was lucky enough to land a role in *The Hot Potato*, an action film set in the sixties starring Ray Winstone. When I got the call from my agent asking if I was interested in going to the casting, I wasn't sure what to expect. I hadn't acted since being at school and had never done it professionally before. But I reckoned the worst thing that could happen would just be not getting the part, and it sounded a fun experience, so I went along to meet the director and producer, who were both big names. I did my audition, left and tried not to overthink it. Minutes later, while I was still wandering down Greek Street in Soho, my phone started to ring. Surely, it couldn't be about the audition – I'd only just left. But it was my agent on the line, congratulating me: I'd got the job! The film was being shot in Belgium and Ray and his wife were complete gems: they really gave me confidence. I was honoured to act alongside Ray. It was only a small role, but it was perfect for me and it really made me fall in love with acting. It's something that I'm hoping to do more of in the future.

As well as these TV and acting jobs, I was a wife and mother: cooking the pasta and the sausage and mash, doing the laundry and the school run, and keeping things running at home twenty-four-seven. I loved spending time with my family, and I always put their needs before my own. I've spent most of my life pleasing everyone else, worrying about being judged and thinking that the right thing for me to do was to be at home, looking after my family. I think this happens to a lot of women when they get married and have children. Deep down, you sometimes wonder *Where did I go?* But I pushed those thoughts away, and thought of my past life as a pop star as somehow 'not reality'. Looking after the house and my family was reality. But now I know I can be both things. I'm a mother, but I'm also a singer and a performer, and whenever I am on stage, I put my heart and soul into my performance. I want to move people. It's what I love and where I feel I can be my authentic self.

By that point, Jamie's career had switched from the pitch to presenting on Sky Sports, and he was also a panellist on the game show *A League of Their Own*. Standing by and watching Jamie become an entertainment star was pretty hard. Don't get me wrong, I was really proud of him – but there was a little, niggling part of me that couldn't help thinking, *That's my world*. Seeing him light up on TV and being able to sense his excitement only served as a reminder of how much I missed that feeling. But that wasn't my world any more. Trying to convince myself that I was happy without my passions was tough. I was never jealous of Jamie's success, but it did make me feel like something was missing.

I'd been asked on loads of reality shows but had always declined the offers. *Strictly* had approached me more than once, but I'd always said no because I didn't want to miss one of the kids' carol concerts, pick-ups or drop-offs, and I wanted to make sure that I was always home to make them dinner. But by 2016, things were different and it felt like the right time. In trying so hard for so long to be the perfect wife and mother, I'd ended up losing my sense of self, and I needed to do something just for me. Saying yes to *Strictly* felt like the most selfish thing I'd ever done, but I knew I needed to make a change in some way. I was struggling. What would any woman do if she was told she wasn't loved any more? I knew I couldn't just continue being at home on my own, worrying about everyone else and my place in the family. My self-esteem was at rock bottom, and I felt so lonely.

I agreed to do the show on the condition that my rehearsals finished at six, which would give me enough time to rush home to cook dinner for the boys. Up until the last two weeks of *Strictly*, I only rehearsed during the day when the boys were at school, and then I'd immediately make the mad dash home. Looking back on it now, it seems a bit crazy, but at the time it's what mattered most to me. I don't think I could have gone through with the show if I hadn't been able to physically be there for my boys.

Once everything was in place, I simply turned up on the first day for a group dance rehearsal, and that was the first time I met everyone. At the launch, I couldn't stop thinking, *I'm not sure if I'm cut out for this.*

Like everyone else, I'd read all the articles speculating about who else might be on the show, but until I walked into the studio that day I was still very much in the dark. The only person who I knew might be appearing was Will Young. He was a good friend whom I respected, and the fact that he was going to be on the show helped me to make my decision to take part.

One of my favourite things about *Strictly* was the routine that evolved around the show. I loved having a purpose every day, and getting in that car each morning to the studio felt brilliant. Although I'd felt a bit rusty at first, it didn't take long to click back into performance mode and I loved the challenge. When you're paired with the professionals, you genuinely don't know who you're going to be put with. I was so happy to be partnered with Kevin, but I had no expectations, and I didn't go into the show thinking I had to take home the trophy. I just knew time was running away and something had to change. The kids were getting busy, Jamie had a very full life of work and social stuff, and I'd been wondering what that left for me. *Strictly* filled that gap.

I was really, really scared to put myself out there again, so it was so lovely to hear comments from women in their forties saying they were proud of me and encouraging me to do my best – that meant a lot. I was still bricking it as each week came around, though! I think it's fair to say that the vibe at *Strictly* is different every year, as so much of it depends on the personalities of the cast. The year I took part, everyone was always excited and dancing backstage. There was a lot of exhibitionism, with partners practising in the corridors before their performance. I, on the other hand, spent all my time in the wings wanting to throw up. I would say nothing and do nothing.

My family loved *Strictly* and were real fans. They would tune in every week without fail and pick their favourites to cheer on each year. I didn't really watch it myself, but knowing that all my family would be thrilled that I was taking part was definitely one of the deciding factors. I knew that they would love it.

It was during my second week on *Strictly* that Grandad Malcolm died unexpectedly at home. He was twelve years younger than my nan, and by that point she had been put into a home as she was suffering from quite advanced dementia. It was hard for all of us, but particularly for my grandad; it broke his heart. He adored her and their love was completely unconditional. He would get up every day and go to sit with my nan in the home for hours and hours, just talking to her and helping her do all sorts of mundane, everyday things, even when she didn't recognise him or know who he was.

On that second week, I was performing the Viennese

waltz to the song 'Hallelujah'. My grandparents had always been quite religious, and I remember thinking that they would have adored the dance. I was in rehearsals when my mum called to tell me that Grandad had died unexpectedly at home due to a massive internal bleed. He had been looking quite unwell for a few weeks, but we'd put it down to him missing my nan and the stress of her illness, not the fact that he himself had been seriously unwell.

I was in the studio when I got the call, and I started crying.

'Are you OK?' one of the producers asked as I hung up, looking concerned.

'My grandad passed away. But I don't want to talk about it,' I said firmly.

'Do you want to go home?' she asked.

'No, let's complete this final couple of hours,' I replied. We never spoke of it again.

I felt completely floored, but I didn't want anyone to know. I didn't want to get a pity vote. Also, I knew that if everyone was nice to me, I would burst into tears – and I did not want to cry on national telly. Having grown up in the industry, I felt it was important to give my all to that dance. I wanted to do it properly and be professional. I didn't want it to be about what had happened that week and for my grandad to become part of the narrative of the show – I wanted to keep the two things separate.

The professionals always have the routine completely locked down before the week starts, so we knew what we needed to do. We practised in the studio every day until we could get the performance as close to perfect as possible. When people think about *Strictly*, they often seem to envisage the couples together for hours and hours on their own, rehearsing passionate dances together while having intimate, meaningful conversations and revealing their deepest, darkest secrets. The reality is that we were very rarely alone, and around ninety per cent of everything we did was filmed by the crew. There was a cameraman, a producer and a runner, so there were at least three other people there for the vast majority of our rehearsal time. They wanted to capture footage for the spin-off shows and cutaways, so they were there ready and waiting in case you fell over or did something stupid – or something really good. So no, it's not hours of sexy tango routines with just the two of you; far from it. I used to spend my rehearsals surrounded by at least three other people, feeling a bit sick and stressed because I thought I didn't know what I was doing.

I enjoyed the fun and banter that came from being with other performers because it reminded me of my old life. On the first show, I stood right at the back, having insisted on wearing a gown that covered me from my neck to my toes. Then, of course, there was the infamous dolly sailor dress. A few days later, Daisy (Lowe) barged into my dressing room as I was getting was changed and said, 'Oh my God, look at your gorgeous body. You have to wear a sexy dress.'

Daisy is a massive supporter of other women, and

she's all about body confidence. She was always trying to make me look sexy and get me to stop covering up. Her saying that was like a shock to the system because I had been feeling so self-conscious about my figure.

And then came 'Flashdance'.

x x x

As the *Strictly* theme tune played, I felt like I might throw up. I was standing at the top of the steps, with Kevin. Pins and needles shot through my fingers, and my heart flip-flopped out of my chest. I was seriously concerned that I wouldn't make it down the steps – my legs had turned to jelly. I tried to inhale deeply, but my breath felt ragged; like I had a vice clamped around my chest.

'Just live it and enjoy it,' Kevin said, all poise.

As I moved into my position on the dancefloor, wearing just a leotard and leg warmers, the studio was so quiet you could hear a pin drop. Touching the floor, my hands felt clammy.

As the first lines of Irene Cara's 'Flashdance ... What a Feeling' blared out, my body naturally reacted to the music, and my fear and anxiety just melted away. I stood up – and I was off. The adrenaline switched from fear to elation in a second. Suddenly, I was in the moment and loving it.

It was my third week of *Strictly*. Having spent the previous two weeks covering up my body with the longest dresses I could persuade the costume team to let me wear, now I was in a black leotard and leg warmers with my whole body on show.

For each dance, there's a certain number of steps and technical elements that you need to incorporate into the routine in order to gain the highest scores. The cha-cha was not my favourite – it was tricky getting to grips with the shape of the dance, and the steps were complicated. Although I'd trained in dance at school, I'd never done ballroom, and during my first few weeks on *Strictly* I had quickly discovered it was a completely different skill. Luckily, I had a few things on my side: I was used to performing, remembering routines, turning and using my arms. I knew I had an advantage in that sense, but the cha-cha felt alien to me – I couldn't work out which way your hips were supposed to go.

The week of rehearsals had flown by and on the Friday I went along to the costume department for my fitting. They suggested I try a leotard to fit with the *Flashdance* theme. The whole costume team were absolutely incredible and always worked so hard to make sure that everyone felt comfortable with what they were wearing. It hadn't taken them long to realise that I preferred being covered up, and they knew a leotard was firmly outside of my comfort zone.

'Absolutely no way,' I said.

But as we talked it through, they told me that, as it was the cha-cha, the alternative was a glittery frou-frou dress, which felt like a world away from what I was used to. That kind of look is just not me at all. The team reassured me that they always used fabrics that were flattering and easy to dance in, and after a little bit of coaxing, I agreed to the leotard. A black leotard and leg warmers really felt like the lesser of two evils. When I tried it on, I realised I would have to find my big girl pants and commit to it.

A lot of the contestants who take part in *Strictly* love the dressing-up aspect of the show and I know some of the outfits are absolutely gorgeous, but that part of it didn't excite me. I only wore fake eyelashes once in twelve weeks, and that was during the Blackpool show when I didn't have the fight in me any more. Generally, I wanted as little hair and make-up as possible. If they bought out a pink lipstick, I would always ask for a nude shade; if they wanted bright eyeshadow, I would suggest a more muted tone. In many ways, I was still trying to hide and be as inconspicuous as possible, even when I was on stage. I wanted it to be about the dancing and not about me.

That Saturday was an exception. I went to the hair and make-up team and Lisa, who was in charge, suggested we do big curls in my hair. It took a couple of hours to do all the styling and it was a complete transformation. When I saw myself in the mirror, I knew that I could do that dance for every girl out there who grew up watching *Flashdance*. The only other option was to hide and shrivel back in to the mindset I'd been stuck in up till now, which was basically dancing but hoping at the same time that no one watched me. I'd grown up adoring *Flashdance* – and now I had my curly head, leotard and leg warmers, and I was dancing to a song that I had literally learned in my living room at the age of ten. Whether that was the week that I was voted out or not, that dance was for every woman who had ever dreamed that one day they would make it on to a stage. It was such a big moment for me.

Looking at the judges beaming and the audience as they clapped along, it was like the positive energy was catching. The steps took care of themselves. It was something about that hair and music – I felt that I had finally left the insecure Louise behind and was back to being the girl who loved performing. It was like I was a different version of me – the one who knew how to put on a great show, not the one who had spent the previous decade in the kitchen trying to make the work surfaces look immaculate and running around after the kids, cooking sausages for their tea. For those two minutes, nothing mattered apart from the performance and the dance. That huge smile was genuine. I was buzzing and I felt truly alive. I knew that it was what I did, what I was best at, and what I really loved.

Even after the 'Flashdance' week, I still wore some quite conservative outfits and much preferred to play it safe. There were weeks when Rob Rinder, who was also performing on the show, would come into my dressing room and say, 'Get those tights off and get that dress shorter. I have had enough of watching you go out there like you don't want to be seen.'

I could feel myself changing, week by week. I was

coming out of my shell and spending less and less time standing in the wings feeling sick. A lot of that was down to the incredible camaraderie, the excitement, the audience, the laughs, and, funnily enough, the nerves. Sometimes I felt like crying, because deep down inside me this voice was screaming, 'This is what I've been missing!'

As far as the professional element of the show went, I don't think I could've done any better. I gave it my all, all the way through. There were no huge dramas and I was thankful for that. I felt so blessed to get high scores, but I always knew there was a level of expectation because I was a trained dancer. Part of my motivation to do well also came from a fear of being in the bottom two following the public vote. As a naturally emotional person, I knew I would find that really hard to deal with mentally, but I count my lucky stars that I never had to face the music. As each week went past, I felt prouder of the fact I was still there.

Musical week, when I performed the quickstep to 'The Deadwood Stage' from *Calamity Jane*, was probably one of my favourites, while another highlight was performing the paso doble in Blackpool. I can't stress enough how incredible it felt to be back on a stage doing something I loved so much. Every week, I found it hard to stop grinning when I danced, as I felt so alive. The paso and the Argentine tango are both moody, sensual dances, so Kevin constantly had to mutter, 'Stop smiling,' to me under his breath, but I just couldn't help it.

The feeling of practising and getting better at some- thing week after week is just amazing for your mental health, even though the scoring can be hard sometimes. I think Craig Revel Horwood was determined to never give me a ten. I saw him about a year later, and he actually told me that I'd made his job very hard. They couldn't just keep giving me high marks, and I under- stood that. It was all part of the show and it didn't bother me. I knew some of the dances I did could have been better – and I knew that some were great.

After every show on a Saturday night, my mum and Jamie's mum would come to watch and I went home with them. During the show's run, I never went out once to a club or a bar outside the green room. My family would always be there, or Jamie, and we would have a few drinks, but I was always exhausted. It was all so physical, and I knew that on the Monday morning I would be back in the studio, learning the dance for the following week. I think the only socialising I did during that time was when Jamie and I went out for dinner or to celebrate friends' birthdays. Otherwise, I was com- pletely focused on and committed to perfecting the routines. After being a mum for such a long time, I had the opportunity to go out there and give it my all – and it felt brilliant.

I also knew the foundations were being laid for me to have a career again. By that point, that fact was very much part of my decision-making. The show reminded me how much the entertainment industry is part of me.

I've always known that I feel my best when I'm getting up on a stage, singing and dancing, but I hadn't realised quite how low I would feel without that in my life. Before *Strictly*, my self-esteem had reached an all-time low, but as the weeks went by, I started to feel more confident. I never stopped wanting to perform.

Approaching the final, all I could think about was the fear of it being over. I was terrified of feeling directionless again. I was in the final three with Ore Oduba and Danny Mac, and as I rehearsed that week, my overriding emotions were worry and panic. I had loved being in *Strictly*, so going back to my old life felt incredibly daunting. The fear of not performing any more sent me into sheer panic. I wasn't worried about who would win, because I didn't for one second think it would be us. I knew it would go to someone who wasn't a trained dancer, so I wasn't disappointed. I was just so happy to be in the final.

The *Strictly* tour started in January, and I let my hair down a bit. I'd only said yes at the last minute, again because I felt torn between being at home and being on the road, but finally I decided to go for it, as it was only for a few weeks. It felt liberating to enjoy some time for myself. Another thing that swayed me was the tour meant that I'd get the chance to perform at Wembley again. I loved the performances – and to be honest, it felt incredible to win. I think between Danny and me, we won twelve shows each on that tour. It was all the fun of the TV show, but with none of the intense pressure.

After *Strictly*, I realised that I couldn't just go back to my life as it had been before. I didn't want to continue running around after everyone else, occasionally promoting a yogurt or doing a little TV presenting job. I wanted to sing. I wanted to perform and get back on a stage in front of an audience.

That's when the shit hit the fan. No one could understand why it was so desperately important to me, but it wasn't like I'd 'discovered' a love of performing and how it made me feel – *Strictly* had been a reminder of everything I was missing. When I look back at that time, I have mixed emotions. I loved being part of the show, but it also came with a lot of unnecessary press intrusion and attention. Some people may say I was a victim of this, but that's not the case. My marriage broke up for many reasons.

It would be impossible to do a show like *Strictly* without forming a professional friendship – you wouldn't be able to dance well with someone you hated; it would make the whole experience utterly miserable. No matter who you are partnered with, you have to enjoy what you are doing in order to do a good job, but that doesn't mean that there is any more to it than the dancing. All the same, I was scared. I had seen the headlines play out before, and no one knows whether what they are reading is true or not. Even on the show itself, when I walked down the stairs after it was announced that Kevin and I were through to the next week, I always preferred to give him a high five rather than hug him.

In the *Strictly* world, I think that came across as quite cold, as everyone hugs, but I felt uncomfortable going beyond the simple high five. It's a job, a role, and a programme. I made lots of friends as the weeks went on, but my closest friendships were with other contestants like Rob Rinder and Daisy. The press kept saying that I was out partying until all hours with twenty-somethings, and who did I think I was? To me, this highlighted the double standards of the press. Jamie would be out with friends who were much younger than him and no comments were made in the press. The truth is that I didn't go out partying a lot. When we were on tour after the show, of course I'd go for a drink with some of the other dancers – we were all staying in the same hotel together. Daisy is a really spiritual and warm soul, and neither of us are party girls. If we did ever go out, it was normally to the theatre or for dinner. We always supported each other, and she was a great friend to me.

It bothered me that so much of the hype around the show isn't even about the dancing. If there was a way to shut down all the gossip, it would be so much better. I found the rumours exhausting and unfair, and there are definitely ways the show could be better for families. For example, if husbands, wives and partners were allowed in the dressing rooms, there wouldn't even be an opportunity for rumours. Also, families could be included far more, which I think would make the experience more enjoyable for everyone involved.

The thing that *Strictly* gave me was a false sense of security. There is an energy around the show that makes you feel invincible. I felt like certain people had my back, and, in hindsight, this wasn't really the case. I was so scared about going back to normal life and losing what I'd achieved on that show. I could have addressed that with Jamie, and told him what I felt I was lacking in my life, and what we could do to move forwards and solve it – but I didn't. Looking back, I wish I'd sat down and really tried to explain how much I was struggling, how unimportant I felt in our lives together and how depressed this made me feel. I wish I'd been honest and said I felt unloved. I never spoke about how things were at home to a single soul. The loneliness had just ebbed into my life, but I ran away from it, refused to face it until it was too late to try to sort it out. If I'd done the show four years earlier, this wouldn't have happened. I wouldn't have walked away from my marriage – I think I would've been too scared and, to be honest, I wasn't in a place where I wanted my marriage to end. *Strictly* gave me a new path; it showed me that I would be OK, and that I could find work again. But I still wish I'd done things differently, because I feel like I hurt a lot of people and I'll always be sorry for that. I just kept running and running. It was like I was watching someone else's life in front of me unravel, and I just couldn't put it back together.

You've Got This . . .

The question 'Are you happy?' is one that some women find particularly hard to answer

Being fulfilled, being true to yourself, and following your passions; these are the things that make you happy. When I was married and people used to ask me how I was doing and what I had been up to, I would lapse into talking about the boys and Jamie, and how they all were. I realised that I focused so completely on their happiness that I forgot my own. I felt like the happiness of my husband and children was a direct result of how well I was doing as a mum and wife.

Women are taught to pour their energy into those around them, nurturing them and their needs. For lots of women, this is their family, but for others, it might be their friends or even their boss or work. I am a natural people-pleaser and in most situations, I slip into this accommodating role, always wanting to make sure other people are happy and putting myself and my own wants and needs at the bottom of the heap. I think being a mum intensifies this instinct, because nothing is more important than our kids.

There is also this idea that we can have it all: that we can be the perfect wife, mother, friend and daughter, and also have a career. In the creative industries, this can be particularly hard and unachievable, so many women, like me, are forced to give up their careers. Also, there is this feeling that once we are mothers, we stop being the person we were before. Men do not seem to have this problem; they remain the same people, with their own lives and identities.

I don't think anything can prepare you for being a mum and that feeling of adoration and love. Of course, whether you go back to work or not, becoming a mother comes hand in hand with a sudden lack of time, as every spare moment is devoted to running around after the kids. After years of having no time to ourselves, our old identities become so buried beneath the piles of washing and ironing, they can become lost.

In relationships, it sometimes feels that there is an expectation that women are around to make men's lives tick

At what stage do we turn around and say, 'I'm not having this. I am as important as you'? Women are good at being selfless. Sometimes, it feels like keeping everything together and running smoothly is just what women do. It's what I've seen my mum do, and I'm sure it's what she saw her mum do. It's just seen as the norm, and I'm not sure that will ever change.

It is so important to keep part of yourself back and continue to do what you love, just for you

I think equality is the most important thing in a relationship, and this means different things for different couples. I understand that many women want – or need – to go out to work, and at the same time, I have many friends who stay at home. For people who stay at home with the kids while their partner works, it's important to recognise and remember that your partner couldn't go and do that job and have that life without you running the ship at home. It would be impossible. It's not about what you put in financially; it is about the ways in which you support each other, practically and emotionally. I did live in a beautiful house and drive a great car, but my responsibility as a wife and a mum was still the same as for any other woman. The love and time I gave to my family, and the importance of me being there for everyone else was still the same; I just did it in a more luxurious way. But I still felt like the lesser party in the marriage – I just wanted to be equal.

I always kept some of my career going, but not enough. Of course, as we go through life, we will always have to give certain things up, but no matter how much you love your children and your partner, I would urge you to always hold a little bit of something back, just for you. You could be married to the best man in the world and have the most amazing kids, but if you completely devote yourself to them, you can forget to look after yourself and what you love. After getting married and having kids, I feel that I very quickly gave everything over to everyone else in my life. I forgot to look after myself and lost part of myself and my identity. Having a balance is part of what makes us happy and our identities and passions are what fuel us in life.

Do you bend over backwards to constantly make everyone else happy while never thinking about what you really want and need?

The start of this process is giving yourself permission to change and reclaim your identity as an individual. I tried so hard at home and poured my life into hoping everyone would appreciate my efforts. I became obsessive about stupid things, like having a spotless kitchen or garden. For years I was that 'yes' person, who did everything for everyone else, even if it didn't make me happy. I think going off and doing *Strictly* made me realise there was more to life than just trying to be this perfect person at home. I fell in love with the show, with feeling loved by the public, with the sense of being part of something. My unhappiness was no one's fault. I had all the material things you could ask for; I didn't want for anything. I just needed my identity again.

Being a mum is the most important job in any family, but if you are at home and feel lost in any way, I would suggest you think about your other talents and skills, away from the home. What do you love doing? What are you good at? What are your interests? I am never going to ever stop putting my boys first, but I think it is good to acknowledge your own passions and interests now and again, and to push back against that feeling of always being at everyone else's beck and call.

I have no idea what is going to happen in the future for me: all I know is that I fought for this and it's something I needed to do

It's taken everything, but pursuing my love of dancing and music is something I need to do for *me*. Does it make me any less of a mum to my boys? No. If anything, being myself and following my passions probably makes me a better parent, because they get to experience me being the best and fullest version of myself. They deserve that person in their lives. It is so important to take care of your own needs – and, ultimately, the choice is yours to make.

Chapter Seven

SPEAK YOUR TRUTH

'A lie can travel halfway around the world while
the truth is still putting on its shoes.'

Anonymous

*L*ooking out of the window in my rented apartment in
Wimbledon, I could see the vehicles lined up against
the pavement. I knew there were photographers inside,
just waiting for me to leave so they could snap a photo.
There were three vans with blacked-out windows and
one car. By that point, I knew the registration numbers
of each one, as they had been following me so closely
for what felt like for ever. I knew they were there, just
waiting, and would sit it out for as long as they needed
to. When they would get bored was anyone's guess. I
felt trapped, like some sort of caged animal and so, so
desperate.

How had my life got to the point where I could no
longer step outside my front door without having a

camera in my face and a story running about how I was an awful mother, that I had left my marriage, that I was to blame? There they were, looking for a photo they could splash with a damaging headline for everyone to read with their coffee and croissant the next morning.

I sank to my knees, crouched down by the radiator, and sobbed and sobbed. That day was the first time that I ever wondered whether I would be better off not being here. The feeling of just wanting to take the pain away was so overwhelming, and I felt completely out of control of everything. I rang Jamie, begging him and pleading with him to help me stop the press attacks. I was completely desperate. Next on the list of who to call was my press lawyer, who put out a note to the papers asking them to respect my privacy. Frustratingly, this had the opposite effect and they simply piled on even harder the following weekend with even more stories, most of which were completely untrue. How could the people that were supposed to protect me be so power-less? I felt like I had nowhere to turn. It was as if my life was simply news fodder: my pain was just idle gossip, something to keep people entertained on the morn-ing commute.

After the split and the fallout of the following weeks, the press had a field day, and I felt like everything was twisted to make me look like the guilty party. They really went for me. I felt as if I was taking bullet after bullet, for everyone and everything, and no one was standing up for me.

But I knew I had to maintain a dignified silence. The idea of speaking out terrified me. I was frightened that someone would use my words to fuel the fire, so I didn't say anything – and it all just snowballed. Every headline and picture felt like a judgement of me as a person.

There was even one set of pictures of me out at a Matthew Bourne ballet with the accompanying head-line: 'Louise spotted out looking cosy with Kevin'. What they failed to mention or photograph was that my mum was there too. Why would I have taken my mum along if we were on some sort of date? It was madness. I had to take a step back from my friendship with Daisy, as it became impossible for me to do anything with her without her somehow being held responsible for my marriage breaking down.

But what I found the most hurtful of all were the comments and articles about the kids. No mum wants people to think she's left her kids, which of course I hadn't. I'd walk over the ocean to protect my boys. I could tell how hard it all must've been for them. I was pretty sure that Charley was reading everything that was being written about me, and even actively seek-ing it out. I was under no illusions about how tough it must have been for him. During those days, I had some really dark thoughts. I would be standing in central London, watching the buses whizz past and I would wonder whether it would be easier for a bus to take me out. All it would take was for me to step out at the wrong moment and it would all be over. I didn't want anyone to feel guilty or to say that it was anyone's fault. But I did feel that low. I knew I wouldn't do it, though. I love my kids too much. I knew – and know – that no matter what anyone thinks about me, my children need me.

Even now, I struggle to vocalise how I felt during that time. I think I will always be nervous about what people write and say about me. I was followed every day, on the school run and to the supermarket, and even though I wasn't doing anything 'wrong' or bad, having cars following me made me feel sick. They followed me into car parks in the hope they would get something, anything, to sell. I felt trapped and it all made me so terribly, terribly anxious. There were days that I wouldn't wish on my worst enemy.

Magazine and newspaper articles can sometimes be the worst, and they always seemed to be illustrated with the worst possible pictures of me, with no mention made of my professional successes. I know many of these publications are edited by women, and I wish they would pause and think about why they are choosing to tear down other women in this way.

Maintaining a dignified silence was tough, but I didn't want to say anything. I'll never lie, because if I lie I will have to hide. I am done with ducking down in the back of a car, so no one sees me. Finally, as time went on, things seemed very slowly to turn around.

x x x

For me, the most important thing about my own health is having a healthy mind. I spend a lot of time in my own head, which is quite dangerous, and I am always trying to remember to look outwards and stop dwelling too much on negative thoughts. When I think back to my marriage, I don't think I realised at the time that my mental health was suffering. I wish I had asked for help then. Twenty years ago, no one spoke about mental health in the way that they do now. Jamie was always really great about the compulsive behaviour that had developed out of my anxiety, and I think everyone just accepted that that was me and that was what I did – I just took a lot longer than some other people to do certain things. I would tell myself if I did these things in a specific way, then I would feel better about something or have a good day the next day. When I did have a better day or things worked out, I would latch on to that as evidence; it was a vicious circle. It's only recently that I have been free of compulsive thoughts, although occasionally something will still pop into my head, and I need to remind myself to see it for what it is.

I have suffered from real periods of anxiety in the past. There was a time a few years before Jamie and I split up, when one of my beloved dogs died in an accident. I really hit rock bottom. I just could not stop crying. I love my animals; they are like people to me and I was devastated. We were away on holiday at the time, and I was so conscious of the fact that I didn't want to ruin it for Jamie and the boys. Our time together as a family was really precious, so instead of telling anyone how I felt, I would sob hysterically in the shower because it was the one place where no one could hear me. Some days, I would go to the supermarket, and on the way I would pull over into a lay-by and just cry uncontrollably. I never told anybody. The only person I could ever really cry in front of was my mum.

I internalised all my emotions; I knew I was upset about my dog, but it felt like I was crying about something much bigger, even though I didn't know what it was. I could never put my finger on it – I just felt so awful and down. Looking back now, I think I was quite depressed, and I can recognise that anxiety was really starting to take over, but at the time I felt like everyone else's needs and emotions were more important than mine. I couldn't admit that I was struggling, especially when life was so good for so many reasons. I was so used to just pretending I was fine. I call it 'tits and teeth': being able to smile, and lift my shoulders back and present myself to the outside world as completely happy and together, even when I felt awful inside. I was a complete pro at that.

However, I did know that something was wrong and that the way I felt wasn't 'normal', so I phoned up my doctor and told him that I couldn't stop crying and needed something to help me feel better. He put me on a course of antidepressants, but when I started taking them, they made me feel worse. I was yawning all the time and felt so lethargic. I was putting on weight and I wasn't myself at all. I hated the feeling, and I guess I wanted to feel OK without them, so pretty quickly I stopped taking them. As I threw the packet of pills away, I thought to myself, *I'm never taking one of those pills again*. Looking back, I probably did this all the wrong way. I know that antidepressants can take a few weeks or months to work, but I quit them quickly, which was probably the worst thing to do.

For a couple of years after that, I pretended I was fine, but I can see clearly now that I wasn't. I got shingles twice in one year and felt dreadful. The first time I was diagnosed, the doctor told me that it was stress-related and warned me to take it easy or make a change in my life. Six months later, it was back, and the doctor said the same thing – that I was clearly very stressed and unhappy, and needed to calm down. I was in denial about how I really felt, though, so I just plodded on. By this stage, I had lost all trust in my own emotions because I was so used to masking how I felt. I could get all dressed up and put on my make-up, plaster a smile on my face and go out, and no one knew. It was a weird feeling, because on the surface, life was great. I had my husband and kids around me and I didn't want for anything financially, so I couldn't explain why I felt like I did. I constantly felt like I was walking a tightrope, and that everything could go wrong at any moment. I found something to worry about in every tiny thing. I could not normalise anything and it felt almost as if life was too good to be true, and I was only one step away from it all going wrong.

Going through my divorce was a massive blow to my mental health, and it definitely took a turn for the worst at that time. Looking back, I don't think I was in a great place mentally before I went into *Strictly*. I was feeling really vulnerable and low. Would I have done that show again if I had the chance? No. Nothing could be worth putting anyone I loved or love through the heartache and the headlines it has caused. It all felt like a circus. If I hadn't been doing *Strictly* at the same time as the divorce happened, it wouldn't have been a 'story' in the same way, and maybe the press would have given me an easier time. As much as I appreciated everything that came out of the opportunity, the bad probably out-weighs the good – but, of course, it is easy to see that with the benefit of hindsight.

x x x

It was the small things I agonised over. I'd established such a routine over the years, and spent so much time thinking about the boys and Jamie, that I'd completely forgotten to think about myself and what I liked. When it came to going to the supermarket, I'd walk around in a daze. As crazy as it sounds, I didn't know what to buy, because I'd forgotten what *I* liked to eat. Simple tasks seemed like such a challenge. Everyday things, like the school run, became impossible for me. It was a real low point in terms of self-esteem and there were points where I didn't feel like I would recover. When I woke up in the morning, I genuinely didn't know how I would get through each day. As embarrassing as this is to admit, I would even sometimes turn on the football when I was at home in my flat. I don't even *like* football, but I had spent twenty years having in on in the background, and I didn't know what else to put on. It was like my internal GPS had been switched off. I just didn't know what to do with myself, and this familiarity was something to cling on to that was comforting.

It's almost like I have no real recollection of that time, emotionally or otherwise: it just feels like a bit of a blur. I was never really present. I have always taken such pride in cooking dinner and sitting down with my boys to eat, but during that period, it was like I wasn't really *there*; I just wasn't in the room at all. All that time came and went, and I somehow got through it, but they were very dark days. It was like watching someone's life rolling in front of my eyes and I just couldn't catch it.

I saw lots of psychiatrists in the months following my divorce, as I knew I was unwell, but I was never open with them about how I truly felt and the reasons for the break-up. I skirted around the issues, so I think it was very hard for anyone to do a proper job with me. Despite knowing that anything I told the psychiatrists was confidential, I never really trusted anyone not to repeat what I had told them. And there was the fact that I didn't really want to face up to my real feelings. I wasn't being honest with them – or with myself, really. I was conscious that a lot of the problems in my marriage were about my emotions and lack of confidence, but I found it very hard to admit this. Often the conversation would turn to antidepressants and the fact that they might help me get through it. I know they work for a lot of people and save many lives, but because of my past experience of them, I didn't want to take them.

After the split with Jamie and the press intrusion that followed, my brother Joe moved in with me for a while. My family knew that I shouldn't be by myself and that I needed to be around people who loved me and understood the situation. After a few weeks with Joe, I moved back in with my mum. The boys and I spent five months on blow-up beds in the living room. My mum was instrumental in helping me get back on track. She gave me a huge amount of time to talk about my feelings and chat through what had happened. One of my friends, Charli, stuck by my side for three months. She is a huge character and we are like chalk and cheese, but she is one in a million. Some days, just putting the music on really loudly in the car and singing along can lift my spirits, and she knew that. She gave up her job and moved in with me, cooked for me and looked after me. I have never needed someone like her by my side more than I did in those times.

One area that has caused me a lot of struggle when it comes to my mental health is social media, and specifically trolling. The problem is this: when life is good and you feel secure and confident, what people say on social media doesn't really mean anything, and it is much easier to ignore. But when life is tough, or you feel down on yourself or anxious, those negative comments seem to simply amplify everything you are already feeling. People often say, 'Just ignore them, or block them, they are just internet trolls!' Every time I hear that, I think I might scream. If I spent all day blocking trolls and hurtful comments, it would be a full-time job. Of course, ignoring them makes complete sense, because trolls are simply looking for a fight or some sort of attention. They are like playground bullies who put others down to make themselves feel better. But what sort of world are we living in where grown adults can write the sort of stuff they do on social media or in the comments sections on websites like the Mail Online? What is it that we need to do to tackle the heart of the problem? I equate reading these comments to a form of self-harm. Trolling has become such a huge issue on social media that we now have the option to remove comments from our posts, so why don't news articles do the same? Many articles seem to be written specifically to incite trolling: headlines about someone's 'amazing' figure just make trolls turn round and say the opposite. If these articles aren't discussing women's bodies, they are focusing on how 'heartbroken' someone is. Why can't these articles champion women instead of pushing them down? We all know those bullies on the playground or in the workplace, but this feels much, much bigger than that.

It feels like bullying on a national scale, and it chips away at you.

On days that I am feeling down about myself, those comments can really hurt. The number of positive comments always outweighs the negative ones, but somehow that doesn't matter. I can't help but focus on the negative comments, and I think that's a problem many of us have. It only takes one nasty dig to completely destroy your confidence, and no number of supportive comments can alleviate that pain. The examples are endless. One night, I got a message that basically said I was a talentless nobody and it's no wonder that Jamie left me. That I was going to die alone while he would find someone a thousand times better than me. I couldn't sleep after reading it. I'm happy to take on board criticism and I don't think I'm perfect, but this kind of comment is just completely uncalled for – and extremely hurtful.

Every set of pictures of me brings with it comments that I am fat, worthless and disgusting. Not that long ago, I was papped doing the supermarket shop while on holiday in Ibiza. There was news that Jamie had a new girlfriend, and I guess everyone was looking for a reaction from me. I hadn't brushed my hair, and had just grabbed Charley's shorts to wear on the way out the door. It was an overcast morning, so it felt like a good opportunity to do some shopping. It just seems crazy to me that this was actually newsworthy. Comments included: 'The size of those legs. Get to the gym,' 'She looks rough,' 'Oh God, she's huge,' 'Talentless and irrelevant,' 'She's pretty fat! She looks terrible,' 'So desperate it's embarrassing,' 'Shapeless lump,' 'Cheap, demeaning, and embarrassing,' 'Nothing special about a stocky fat little hamster, she needs to grow up, Jamie ain't coming back.'

I could go on. This is not just one or two people; there were over 600 comments, sitting under pictures of me buying groceries on holiday – pictures that I hadn't asked anyone to take.

A week or so before that, I'd had pap shots taken of me when I was out with some friends. The lighting was bad and the angles were awful. I think they were taken from a boat on the Thames but I certainly hadn't been aware of any photographers. Again, the comments were awful: 'Wow, she looks as rough as a Brillo pad,' 'Rough-looking, is she ill?' 'Embarrassing,' 'She looks good next to the rubbish bin. Right environment,' 'Legs like hams' . . . it goes on. I was just out trying to enjoy my evening. I mean, why are people even interested? But more important than that, who are these grown adults that write this stuff, and at what point are we going to stand up and say no, enough is enough?

These articles and the comments that go with them are almost always about women – our figures, our perceived physical flaws, what we are wearing, or how we have gone wrong in our relationships. Sometimes is it even worse than trolling, and slips into misogyny. I am called awful names and attract unwanted sexual comments. I know many women in the public eye suffer far more, receiving threats of violence. These types of comments would give anybody nightmares. This behaviour is vile, upsetting and inexcusable.

You've Got This . . .

I think that everyone struggles with their mental health to some degree at some point in their lives

I know they say that one in four people suffer with mental health issues, but I honestly feel the figure is much higher. No one is superhuman or invincible, and every person has their own struggles, or may be very close to someone who suffers. Just because someone may appear to have 'everything' on the outside, don't think that it means they are immune. Even though we are becoming more aware of and more open about mental health as a society, there is still a long way to go.

I have learned that it is never a good thing to hide how you truly feel

If the people around you are not willing to be by your side when you really need them, then you need to be with different people.

I have learned that hiding how you feel or covering it up is the worst thing you can do. I always internalised and pushed down my feelings – I was the queen of bottling everything up. I think this just compounded how I was feeling and made things even worse, because these feelings have to come out at some point. By trying to deny my emotions, I simply made myself feel worse for longer, because I wasn't facing up to how I really felt about something.

Luckily, I can be open with my mum and my friends. It is so important to talk about how you feel – and other people can only help you if you tell them what's going on. Sometimes, even when I am saying something about how I've been feeling, I know that I might sound irrational, but my friends accept it and let me share what I need to, and then we talk it through. There is absolutely no weakness in being honest and open about how you're feeling, however small or insignificant you perceive your problems to be. Talking about your feelings is the only way you can begin to understand them – and it definitely makes you feel less alone. No one would ever suggest not getting help with a physical problem like a broken leg, and mental health is no different.

I have always found it very difficult to open up and trust people, but if you are struggling, I urge you to try to find someone you can confide in. I don't think there is any right or wrong person to talk to – it's different for everybody. For me, it has always been my mum and my friends, but if you would rather not talk to a friend or family member, try a therapist or your GP. More recently, I have found great comfort in talking to a spiritualist, who has helped me unpick certain parts of my life and understand why I feel the way I do about them. The more I talk about it, the more I feel I have control over how I am feeling, and my own ability to change my mindset. As well as talking about it, I know some people find it helpful to write down how they are feeling.

Loneliness is more common than we think

There are very few people who go through life without feeling lonely at one time or another. I admire people who can be on their own and who love going on holiday on their own. If you can be comfortable in your own space and head, that is fantastic.

Social media does not tell the truth. I've read that those people who use social media the most are lonelier than others. I sometimes feel that the more I post on Instagram, the less happy and fulfilled I am. People might say, 'You look great and like you are having a fab time,' but this is far from the truth. When I don't post for a long time, it probably means that I am in a better place emotionally. Remembering that, and having boundaries around social media and how you use it is healthy.

Not everyone is a good listener who will make you feel better when you are struggling

I have learned that if people can't accept you at your best and also at your worst, then it is OK to cut them off. I know this is much easier said than done. I worry so much about being unkind to others and saying no, but I am slowly realising that if a relationship is to the detriment of my own mental health, it can never be worth it. You should never have to change yourself to please another person or prove your worth. I am slowly learning to stand up to negative people and cut them out of my life.

You must protect yourself and your own mental health first and foremost

It is so important to be kind to yourself. Of course, there are many practical things you can do to protect your mental health. For me, playing the music that I love at top volume or simply taking some time out can instantly lift my spirits. For some people, I know journaling, meditation, exercise, or just calling a friend can do the same for them.

They say that going through a divorce is one of the most stressful life events you can experience

It was such a sad time for me and definitely the toughest thing I have ever had to go through. With any separation or break-up, there is so much to think about on a practical level as well as an emotional one. My world was turned completely upside down in every way, and I doubted every part of myself. It is important to never go through anything like this alone. Being strong doesn't mean not crying or not asking for help. It is so important to talk about things, and sharing your feelings with others is the first step to moving forwards.

How can we create a culture of kindness online?

I feel like we need to change the context in which we consume media, because the current system just encourages clickbait – and the more people look, the more these kinds of stories will appear. Cruelty feels like a key part of celebrity culture, and all people in the public eye, including female politicians, seem to face some sort of abuse as part of their everyday lives and are expected to just suck it up. And people believe so much of what they read. I talk about kindness a lot, and I think that's because I have experienced such spite and malice. Everyone is swept up in their own busy lives, and we forget how important it is to be kind.

I think we can all play a small part in this change. Before you post on social media or write something in the comments under an article, it is always worth thinking: 'Is it true? Is it necessary to write this? Is it kind?' I would love to see tougher obligations from social media platforms, and news articles with the comments switched off. I would love for picture editors to illustrate stories with nice photographs, not the worse ones they can possibly find, and I would love to see journalists writing stories about women without commenting on their figures. Present the facts by all means, but do it in a way that is both fair and kind.

I would love to live in a world where this kind of bullying behaviour is not tolerated

I know of many women who suffer due to trolling. Caroline Flack was a great friend of mine, and she was the most warm-hearted and fun person. She lit up every room she went into with her warmth and energy, and her smile was dazzling. After she died, we all talked about being more kind to each other and the hashtag #BeKind snowballed. It felt like there was a widespread call to be kinder, both on- and offline, because you never know what someone is really going through. For a few days, it felt like something really might shift, and that perhaps people were starting to take stock of the true impact that our online behaviour can have. But the world kept turning, and still the trolling and bullying continues; it seems the world of online news and social media has moved on to a different topic or mission. I don't feel like much has changed. We need more than just platitudes and empty words. How many more people will die before there is real change? Online spaces might be a place for free expression, but they're also often fertile ground for bullying, boorishness and cruelty. There are many people out there who are written about in this way and they are deeply unhappy. Something needs to change, and it needs to happen now.

The good days will outnumber the bad

If you are going through a hard time and struggling with your mental health, remember that everyone has good days and bad days; you just need to get to a stage where the good ones outnumber the bad. There are up and downs, and some days feel like you are taking ten steps backwards and none forwards. It is absolutely OK to have days like these or moments that you don't show up. This does not define you. Your mental health and the challenges you are facing are not who you are: they are something that you are experiencing. Your feelings are always valid, no matter how things look from the outside. Sometimes hitting rock bottom is not the worst thing that can happen, because from there, you can only move forwards and upwards. There are times when I felt that this would never happen for me, but slowly and surely, I am emerging, stronger than ever.

Chapter Eight

BE PROUD OF WHAT YOU DO

'Nothing is ever wrong. We learn from every
step we take. Whatever you did today was the
way it was meant to be. Be proud of yourself.'
Anonymous

'*I*'m gon' make you work out,
  if you wanna work my body ... '
   I was sitting in a dark room as the beat began to play
and the screen in front of me lit up. It was March 2019,
and the first time that I was seeing the video for my
new single, 'Stretch'. Two video directors, my video
commissioner and my manager were watching it. I
had spent hours making decisions around the video,
and obviously I'd been there as we shot it, but you
don't really know what it looks like until you see it on
a screen, the idea is still only in your own head. There
was a slight buzz of nervous energy in the room. The
stakes were high; I knew everyone wanted me to love

it. I could feel my heart racing. I wanted it to be so good and everything that I imagined that it could, or would, be. I knew this was the first time that people would be seeing me doing music in nearly twenty years. It could not be wishy-washy or just 'nice'. It needed to be impressive, bold and strong. I've been described as 'nice' for my whole life; and that is simply not me. I am passionate, kind, emotional. I wanted this video to convey all those things.

As the video started, the first thing I noticed was the massive scar on my chin from where I had fallen over a few weeks beforehand. But I quickly moved past that, and I could see myself strutting around the set with all the sass in the world. I knew this song would be the opener to my new album *Heavy Love* and in that moment, I wanted to cry. I just felt so proud of myself. It wasn't because I thought I was great – it was because, no matter what anyone had thought or said about me over the previous few years, I had followed my passion, and here was the result of all that hard work. I'd gone from being in a place where I thought that my life was over to strutting my stuff just as I had two decades ago. It felt like whatever had happened, I hadn't held back – I'd given this album my very best shot. I might have held back from saying certain things in interviews, but in these songs, I had poured out my heart and bared my soul: and this was the result.

I adored the process of making the video for 'Stretch'. A lot of people don't realise how much control you can or can't have over music videos. I've been doing this for a long time now, so it's amazing to finally get more freedom to make my own choices about my music career; it's just about the only part of my life where I am in charge. Of course, I also have people around me who are more experienced and whose opinion I really value, so my management and A&R make choices around singles and other stuff. They're the experts when it comes to what is getting picked up and what radio stations are playing, so I'll often take their lead and the whole process is a real team effort.

But I had a clear vision for this video, so I sent my video commissioner, Marisa, a mood board that encapsulated the look and feel I was going for, and she sent me three treatments from potential directors. Each director brought something unique to the table: one was a massive name; another was someone I'd worked with before, who had also done some huge videos; and the final treatment was from an unknown German couple who were both just twenty-three years old. The video is such an important part of the process, so I really took my time reading the treatments and looking at the visualisations of how each director thought the video could be shot. One of my key concerns was the lighting: you can have the best director in the world, but if the lighting isn't right, it's all a waste of money.

'I think I want to go with the German couple,' I told Marisa eventually.

Marisa laughed. 'Nine out of ten people would have

probably just gone with the famous guy, or opted for the director whose last video was with Beyoncé – but you're going with the two unknowns. It shows you understand the business.'

We chuckled.

'I mean, sure, they're just starting out now, but I can guarantee that in twenty years' time, they'll be massive names,' I said.

When you find up-and-coming talent, you can just feel the raw passion and hunger. And having been in their position myself, I knew they wouldn't take anything for granted. Sophia and Robert had absolutely nailed what I was looking for. Robert even took over the camera himself at one point so that he could get exactly the shot he needed – he was so committed to capturing and being true to the essence of the song. That's what you need: a team that is as passionate as you for something to succeed, and I felt like I had that with *Heavy Love*.

The video finished and the lights came back up. There was a brief pause and, because I'm not one to say, 'Wow, I'm just amazing,' the others stood there with bated breath, waiting to see what I thought.

'I think it's really good. I think? Do you think?' I stammered, grinning from ear to ear.

'It's brilliant,' my manager Wayne said, as we high-fived. I was on my way back.

✗ ✗ ✗

In the dark days and weeks following the break-up of my marriage, my life felt like it was spiralling out of control. Looking to the future was terrifying, but I knew that I had to re-establish my career. So, when I was offered the role of Sally Bowles in a touring show of *Cabaret*, directed by Rufus Norris, my friend Charli, who had been by my side since my break-up, forced me to take the job. She knew how much I wanted to perform in a show.

The role of Sally allowed me to play out this messed-up woman on the stage. Rufus actually said to me, 'You're so good at that role because of what you're going through. You play that role with such sincerity because you're hurting so much yourself.'

It was a real honour to work on the show and take on such an iconic role. It also felt really special acting alongside Will Young, who is an incredible performer. If I could pick any musical to run on the West End, it would be *Cabaret*. It's the only show I know where the curtain goes down and, because the story is so sad, no one applauds. It is so eerily quiet afterwards.

It was tough because it was a touring show, so sometimes I didn't see my kids for four or five days in a row. The press kept saying stuff about how I had gone off working and left the boys with their dad. I was made to feel that being in the theatre was not a job for a mother, and that only a bad mother would choose to go away on tour. But it was a step towards reigniting my career, and the children were growing up – Charley was a teenager by then. People might have said I was off chasing fame, but the truth of the matter was that I was in a shit hotel in Milton Keynes, and the job was for twelve weeks, not twelve years. It was an opportunity that I knew I needed to take. Looking back, I wonder how I ever coped emotionally during that period.

With *Cabaret*, I was given another taste of performing, and it was then that I decided to get back into making music. I was fortunate that my management was very much music management. It's very hard to make good music without the right people. I'm not somebody who can sit in my basement and write, record, play all the right instruments, and produce my album myself. Due to my management, opportunities were arising for me to go to LA and Sweden and work with different writers and music producers. I got a music publishing deal with Warner Chappell and I started writing my new album. Paul Smith, who is my publisher and was a great supporter of getting me back out there, pushed me and helped me. Those people who knew me best could see that I needed to write an album – on so many levels.

I funded my own album because I didn't want to answer to anyone else when it came to my music. If you can own your own material in the music industry, it's such a huge advantage. It means if I ever want to do a Greatest Hits album, or something like that, it would cost nothing for me to put together. I was fortunate enough to be in a position to be able to do this. Rather than spending the money I'd earned on decorating the house or holidays, I decided to invest it in my music. It was a gift to myself, and doing it this way just felt right to me. The record company also probably saw the potential of me making a really honest, heartfelt album if I was allowed to go away and just be creative. They believed that the album could mean so much more than just twelve songs on a disc.

How does the process of being in the studio work for me? When it comes to writing music, it's like something just tingles inside me when the music starts. What I tend to do is work with someone who is great with words, as I'm more about the melodies. Ideally, there will be two or three of us in the studio. Someone will put a beat down, just a simple base line or drum beat, and over that I'll find a melody or rhythm. We find a catchy bit that will sit across the chorus – this is what we call the 'hook'. Then we'll extend out the melody and add the words. My writing is very much a reflection of how I'm feeling that week, or in that moment in time – it's all about the here and now.

I remember one week when I had the right hump. One lyric was, 'I need you like a hole in the head, a wet cigarette, a nightmare in bed ... ' It was all coming out. That didn't make the cut! Because, ultimately, I wanted the album to be uplifting and a source of positive energy. During the writing process, I'd drawn on so many different emotions and aspects of my life, so really it maps the process of me finding myself again.

When I penned 'Breaking Back Together', I'd had such

a tough morning. Even now, I find the mornings tough. I hate them, I don't know why. It's that moment when you first open your eyes and it takes you a couple of seconds to remember your life, where you are and what you're doing. For a few seconds, it's comforting and blank, then the heaviness sets in. For a while, I really struggled, and my mum said she could always see how I was feeling when I came into the room first thing in the morning: she could just look at me and tell whether or not I had that day in hand. We spent a lot of time talking, and she would say, 'I know you are breaking at the moment, but sometimes you need to break apart to break back together again.'

It had been such a horrible time, and there were moments when I felt like I just couldn't cope. I felt like such a failure. But I wasn't going to just dwell, I needed to channel all of those feelings into my lyrics so that I could find light in the darkness

I was writing music for *Heavy Love* for over eighteen months, which is quite a long time in music and album terms. Even though Eternal was amazing, and we wrote so much of *Always & Forever*, when I left it was what I call 'fast pop.' It was always a fast turnaround, ready to start touring and ticking boxes, and I couldn't have done that on *Heavy Love*. But what I did have on my side were the life experiences, and I poured all that emotion and knowledge into the album. I put my soul out there, more than I had ever done before. Before that point, I'd been very protective of my personal life and how much I gave away when it came to how I was really feeling. I had this 'film of perfection' around my life – and that film had been ripped away tenfold. I was a broken mess while writing *Heavy Love*, but I think writing it helped me to process some of my emotion. It was such a cathartic experience, and it was my way of telling my own story. Throughout the album, I took all of my frustrations and the negativity that had been plaguing me and turned it into something that I was so proud of. What you're good at and what makes you feel alive is different for everyone, but for me it's always been music. You know in your soul what it is that feels right for you – always make time for your passions, because you'll feel so much better for it. I wrote about fifty songs, and we only used sixteen in the end: twelve on the album and another four on the deluxe edition. It was such a labour of love and involved a lot of travel, but I got to work with so many incredibly talented people.

After such a long break from the music industry, I felt like I needed to re-establish my sound and what I was about. I wanted the album to be a nod to what people knew me for, but with an added dose of real-ness. 'Villain' is one of my favourite tracks – I feel it has the old Janet Jackson vibe. I also love 'Wrong'. I just wanted to make sure that there was a bit of everything on there, including some really upbeat, inspiring numbers.

It was a great record, but it was strange to realise that it was a total outlier in the charts – from top to bottom, they are full of fresh faces and debut albums, with everyone looking out for the next big thing. You spend so much time working hard to get where you want to be, and I think most young musicians think there comes a time when they've made it and they can kick back and enjoy their success, but the truth is that there are always going to be new hurdles to overcome. For me, and for 'Stretch', it was about accepting that only certain stations were going to play it, no matter what it sounded like. In a way, it would have been so interesting to put out the song with an unknown artist to see what the reaction to it would have been.

'Stretch' wasn't about anything in particular that had happened in my life – it was just a fun song. It was a little bit sexy, but there's no harm in that. It felt really empowering and it was a fun, funky number to launch the album with.

I knew it was important to get the right look for the first video and the album cover, as they were going to set me off on a road I'd be on for the next few years. For the album shoot, I wore a bra top with a man's over-sized leather jacket. One of my friends worried with me about whether it was the right look, as she felt it was a bit too sexy, but it's what I wanted to do. I haven't had my breasts enlarged, or any surgery on my face. With me, what you see is what you get. It wasn't about trying to be sexy – I wanted to look fierce and own my music. I did not want to be in a pretty dress with flowers: that wasn't me. I just wanted to create as much sass as I could muster. For me, that album cover and the video both said, 'Don't mess with me.'

It's always hard to try to establish your career again after a long break, regardless of the industry. And for women in particular, there can be so much judgement – it really doesn't matter what you're doing or who you are, someone always seems to have an opinion. At times, it can be hard to block out the voices that are trying to bring you down. When I decided to release music again, people were quick to form opinions. Some said I was desperate to stay in the public eye, others said that I should stay at home and look after the kids – it was really hard to cut through all the noise. I know a lot of women who have had successful and fulfilling careers feel the same. Why aren't we allowed to still dream, to set goals for ourselves? Why did people think I was having a midlife crisis, because I was getting divorced and trying to carve out a career for myself again? Why was it so hard for everyone to accept that I'd taken time out to look after my kids, and now I felt ready to get back into music? When Jamie and I got married, we were both intensely career-focused, and I understood his passion for football because I felt the same about music. So why, twenty years later, was I being seen as an awful person for having the same aspirations I'd had as a twenty-year-old? I guess what I'm trying to say is that there isn't an expiry date on your ambitions and dreams.

I hadn't toured in a long time, so I thought it would be good to start with a small tour. I was so nervous about putting myself out there again, and to be honest, I was worried that if I chose larger venues, they wouldn't sell out. We decided to schedule the first live show – and my first in fifteen years – at Under the Bridge on Fulham Road. I'd told everyone close to me about the show, hoping they could all come out and support me, and I remember being in the car when I got a call from one of my friends. She'd tried to book a bunch of tickets online, but the website hadn't been working. Hearing that, I was really annoyed and pissed off; I mean, how ridiculous would I look if not a soul turned up because they couldn't even buy tickets? I called my manager, Wayne.

'Yeah, Lou, they're sold out.'

'What?' I replied.

'Yep, they sold out in three minutes.'

I was thrilled and excited, but mainly stunned, because I still doubted myself. Even as we arrived at the venue on the day, I kept asking Wayne what would happen if no one turned up.

'Lou, it's sold out!' he laughed.

When the boys came to see me perform for the first time, Charley said to me: 'Hey, Mum. I didn't realise you were that good. That was amazing.'

That meant the world to me. It was like all of a sudden, something had clicked, and he understood why I had been away working and why I needed to do it. No matter what you do, it's hard not to let the self-doubt creep in sometimes. But there are always those magical moments when someone you love lets you know just how special you are and you feel on top of the world.

After the success of the show on the Fulham Road, I played four more venues as part of my *Intimate & Live* tour. Touring has always been so much fun for me, so I played at the Isle of Wight Festival, too, and at the Pride festivals alongside Britney Spears. The Pride festivals, as always, were incredible; those audiences have stuck by me through thick and thin throughout my career. Performing at Pride, I knew I could be me and feel confident, and I felt so lucky to have that. But being back performing was brilliant, full stop. Looking to see who else is performing, doing the soundcheck, being backstage; it's all such a thrill for me.

While I was writing the album, I was offered the role of Violet Newstead in *9 to 5: The Musical*. I think for anyone who's ever been into the performing arts, the West End is like a golden ticket. Ever since I'd been a little girl, I'd dreamed of making it on to a West End stage, but I was also nervous about working alongside seasoned pros. I couldn't help worrying about what other people might think. I didn't want to seem like a newcomer who was there to take over the show – that was the opposite of what I wanted to do! Ultimately I decided that it was silly to give up on an opportunity without even seeing if I was capable of it first. So much of getting out there again was reminding myself that I *could* do it, and that I needed to stop second-guessing myself.

So I threw myself into it. And once I got over my

worries about what the rest of the cast thought, I felt super proud to be involved. Being dyslexic causes me a lot of grief when it comes to learning lines. I was on the stage for almost the entire two-hour show and I was behind everyone else on learning the script. I knew I'd get there, but I could sense that everyone was apprehensive about whether or not it would happen. To be honest, I was pretty crap during some rehearsals. I had no idea how to manage my dyslexia and anxiety. The more I forgot, the more anxious I felt, and the fewer lines I picked up. After a good few weeks of trying to work out why my lines weren't sticking, Evan, the fantastic director, helped me learn them alongside actions. I worked out that once I associated a line with a particular action, it would be in my brain – and once the words were there, they were stuck in there for good. Now, I think I could perform the whole show, having not done it for six months, as if I had done it last night. In life we're often challenged and pushed to our limits, but we're almost always equipped with the tools to make it through. You just need to dig deep within you.

When I am performing, something happens and everything clicks into place. I would forget so many of my lines in rehearsals, but when it came to the performances, I just didn't. I know everyone around me was worried, but as soon as I stepped out on stage, I would go into performer-Lou mode. There was only one occasion, when I was trying really hard not to cough, and my brain seemed to be so focused on that that my lines slipped from my mind, and I needed a prompt from the sides. Other than that, it went fine.

Ten days before the show opened, I fell and hit my chin while I was rushing up some stairs with the boys' school bags. It sounds really weird, but it was just one of those random things.

Before I went to hospital, I kept telling everyone I would be OK with just a plaster. 'It's fine,' I insisted. 'I can definitely still do *9 to 5*.'

Wayne was on holiday and when I told him about the accident, he was convinced that I was winding him up – so much so that he asked me to send him a picture of my chin. I'm sure as soon as he saw the photo, he'd wished he had never asked. My chin was gaping open and blood was running down my neck.

'Lou, you have cut your chin to the bone. You're not going on stage any time soon!' he told me.

In the end, I needed ten stitches and I had to delay going into the show for three months, but I believe there's always a reason for everything. Looking back on it now, I probably needed that time to get better at what I was doing and understand how it all worked. At first, I was devastated, and spent a few weeks sitting on my sofa eating chocolate biscuits and feeling very sorry for myself, but I think it all turned out OK in the end. A few days before I started my run, we rehearsed together as a cast. It was a tough environment to walk into, as the cast were having to rehearse with me on what would have been their day off. Understandably, many of them probably had better ways to be spending their free time. But I was so grateful for the opportunity, so I worked as hard as I could. My picture was on the poster, so I had to just get on with it.

I did six months of seven shows a week. It was exhausting, but even on the days where I felt tired and drained, once I was on the stage, I loved it. I don't think I ever once pulled into the Savoy Theatre and didn't feel delighted to be there. Some nights, I wanted to well up when I walked out with the rest of the cast to take our bows. There was such a sense of achievement.

One of my key considerations whenever I agree to a job is how long I'm going to be away from home and the kids for, so I was lucky that the producers, ATG, allowed me to do six-week runs of the show, across a period of six months. Originally they had wanted me to do a certain amount of weeks and then the tour, so I rang the executive producer and explained that I was completely committed to the show, but I really couldn't spend all that time on the road. While Jamie and I co-parented, I still wanted to be there for my boys. I think everyone appreciated my honesty and ultimately agreed that they would still work with me. For anyone who's looking to get back into work, it's important from the outset to be clear and honest with what you can and can't take on. Most of the time, employers try to be understanding and adaptable, but you do have to take the first step, put yourself out there and ask. When you make requests like this, you're not being demanding: you're still going to get the job done, you're just saying you might need a little more flexibility.

My stint on the West End was a complete shift from making music: it's not about individuals, but how you work as a larger team. Abiding by certain rules was new territory for me: not out of arrogance, but just because I'd been a solo artist for so long. I'd become quite naïve when it came to what was expected of me. There was one day where a meeting was called about being late, and the fact they wanted the whole cast to be there for the warm-up. I didn't always do this: I was older than the others, and didn't really want to be rolling around the floor stretching. I'd always opted to warm up by myself in my dressing room, but I hadn't realised how this might appear to everyone else. To me it was just one of those things, but I'm not sure everyone else felt the same. Somehow, I'd managed to miss that email, so I had no idea that this meeting was taking place. As I arrived at the theatre, the whole cast was on the stage and the company director was wrapping up the meeting.

'Thanks for all coming, and let's try to always be on time from here on in,' he was saying.

I had come straight from the studio, walking in in my heels and long coat. 'Hi everyone!' I said. 'Sorry, what have I missed?'

'Er, we've just had a meeting about everyone being late,' laughed my co-star, Amber.

I had missed it all – and done exactly what I wasn't supposed to. It was one of those horrible moments of realisation. I've always been that person who's in a bit of a mad rush: the mum that's making bacon sandwiches for her kids five minutes before leaving the house. It's one thing to be late for the soundcheck at one of my own performances, but in the theatre they could have definitely sacked me for being late. Lesson learned. After that faux pas, I knew to always make it in for warm-up, and I learned that I had to be a team player. It is about the whole cast, both on and off stage. You rely on one another a huge amount, and that's a lovely thing because it fosters a sense of camaraderie. There's nothing like taking a bow at the end of the show and people standing up to applaud you because they've just had a great two hours, where they have laughed and cried and felt your emotion. It's got to be one of the most rewarding things about performing.

I had my *Heavy Love* tour all planned out, complete with a live band and full production, and was then supposed to be back in *9 to 5* until the summer. And then the UK was locked down due to coronavirus. That was a real curveball. At the time of writing, I'm not sure whether or not *9 to 5* will come back next year due to the pandemic, but I would jump at the chance if it did. I would also love to do something new in the West End. I did have the chance to perform a socially distanced gig at the Clapham Grand – it was brilliant that we managed to pull it off and, although it was a completely different experience to anything I've been used to, it was thrilling to be back on stage.

I have a long working life in front of me. I have to work and be my own boss because I don't want to have to ask anyone for anything. I don't have anyone to fall back on. I've always had a partner who's the main breadwinner and now I am single, I sometimes think to myself, *How do I maintain this?* I think a lot of us reach a point where we're content, but then the question is, how do you maintain that lifestyle? We all go through ups and downs, and have to overcome setbacks, but the key thing is to face every challenge head-on and keep looking forwards.

It's the promise of the future that motivates me and keeps me striving to do my best. While writing this book, I've been back in the studio. My new work is not going to be about heartache and difficult emotions. There will be no songs about insecurity and feeling down. I just want to make great music, with songs that are empowering and make you want to dance. This next album is going to be in two halves – first, the upbeat bangers that you have to dance to and love every moment of; then the second section is going to be as sexy as it gets. We'll see what everyone says about that – I'm sure they will have an opinion. But you know what? Let them think what they want. I'm just going to do me.

You've Got This . . .

It is impossible to have it all

People say that women can have fantastic careers, a happy husband, an immaculate home, quality time every day with their children, meaningful friendships with plenty of nights out, a well-groomed image and a great family. But really, what woman has it all? You may look at a super-successful woman in the public eye and wonder what her secret is, but the truth is that everybody has to forgo something. You either have a massive career and sacrifice part of your personal or family life, or you move away from doing one kind of work to do another, and so lose what perhaps might have been if you continued on your original path. There is no 'right' path for any woman. We all try to kid ourselves that if we work hard enough or try harder that we might succeed in spinning ten plates successfully at the same time, but if you tried to name five women who genuinely 'have it all' across any industry, you would be hard pushed. It is a bleak and impossible goal. Ultimately, all of us exist in days that are only twenty-four hours long. I feel like women are forced to choose which area they want to focus on, but woe betide us if we make the 'wrong' choice.

When it comes to careers versus family, it is natural for women to feel guilty

I don't ever remember Jamie packing his bags to go to Vegas for five days and asking if we would be all right. I only have to go out for a few hours and I am stressing about whether the boys have everything that they need and telling them when I will be back. Then I step away and feel such guilt for putting myself first. I hate to compare men and women, but the fact remains that women are somehow expected to have it all and be everything to everyone – and that is just impossible. The thing about 'having it all' is that it means you are also 'doing it all'. Even in a world where the domestic load is more equal, at least on a physical or practical basis, the mental stuff, like thinking about birthdays, food and other household things, is still mostly taken on by women. That means women are still taking on a percentage of their partner's fair share of household tasks, on top of doing their jobs and looking after the family.

Whatever it is you want to do, do it for yourself and be proud

Whether your dream is to start up your own business, have a part-time job or focus on being at home, do it for yourself, and be proud of your choices. I have loads of friends who are at home and love being with their families, and I know as much as anyone that that is the hardest job there is. Finding what it is that makes you tick is key. It doesn't matter what other people are doing or what they think about something.

Here in the UK, I don't think we celebrate our successes enough. We tend to underplay everything because we don't like to seem as if we're showing off, big-headed or up ourselves. In our culture, if someone tells us something we've done is amazing, we usually brush off the compliment and mention something we think we did wrong. In America, it's completely different: people are comfortable talking themselves up. I can't get my head around the idea of someone saying to me, 'That show was amazing; you were great,' and instead of me saying, 'Well next time I need to do X, Y, or Z differently,' just smiling and replying, 'Yeah, thanks, I know, I was.' The day I can do that will be a huge success for me!

Celebrate the small successes

Sometimes we don't take pride in our success because we think it may not last. It's as if we're afraid that feeling proud of what we've achieved might somehow jinx it for the future. We need to be proud, here and now, for what we've done in that moment, even if it's something small. We find it easy enough to dwell on small mistakes, so why can't we celebrate our small wins in the same way? I know some things may not feel like an achievement, but they should be treated as one. Had a good meeting at work? Done a good exercise class? Whatever it is, acknowledge it, even if it is just in your own mind. This shift in thought will always lead to bigger things.

It is important to know that when you decide to say yes to one thing, you are allowed to say no to something else

There is no shame in saying no. Ultimately, you can only follow your gut and do what is best for you. If that means you have to restructure your life in some way, then that's what you must do. For me, making *Heavy Love* was such a proud moment. Whatever was going on in the rest of my life, that album was something I wanted and needed to do for myself. If you love what you do and are passionate about it, you will never view your 'job' as work. It doesn't always have to be fun, but focusing on something you are passionate about will mean you feel happier and more contented.

If you never even try something, you automatically forfeit the opportunity to succeed at it

I knew I had to get back into music. When I made *Heavy Love*, I was at such a low point in my life that I felt like I had failed anyway – but I did know I could make music, and I clung to that. The key thing to realise is that if you don't try, you'll never know.

Take stock and remind yourself of what you did and why you did it

People take career breaks for many different reasons. Some people, like me, take a deliberate step away to focus on their families, but there are many other reasons. I'm not going to lie, it can be hard to get back out there after a career break, but it is not impossible. For me, the trigger was *Strictly*, because it reminded me of what I love to do. Know what you want, even if it's currently just a picture in your mind. Think about what the next period of your career could look like: this might spur you on to take the first steps. I spent a lot of time on my album, because I feel that, when it comes to reigniting a career, it is worth giving it time and thought. You don't want to just jump into the first thing that comes along, then regret it later. It's always worth taking the time to look at the end game. I think putting yourself 'out there' and connecting with the right people is key, whether they are recruiters, people in your industry, or others you have worked with in the past. You never know who might be able to help you.

We are always learning, no matter what job we do

I learned some really important lessons when I was doing *9 to 5*. No matter what your job is, I think it's important to remember to be open to change. Regardless of what you do and how successful you are, there is always something new to learn. We might get to an age when we think we should know it all, but the truth is we never do. It's OK to not know everything, whatever age you are.

There may be a lot of distractions from your goals

Seeing the ground that other people have covered in the time that you have been away may be intimidating, or you may worry that your old industry is not one for you any more. Always try to have people around you who you trust and who believe in you. Your talent is still there. Remember: never give up!

Chapter Nine

THERE IS ALWAYS A
SECOND CHANCE

'Life always offers you a second chance. It's called "tomorrow".'

Anonymous

I haven't done this for twenty years,' I laughed as we pulled into my drive in the taxi.

The sun was up and it was eight o'clock in the morning. I waved at one of my neighbours as they took their dog out for a morning walk.

I was performing in *9 to 5*, and I'd been out after the show with my co-star Amber Davies and one of the hairdressers from the hair and make-up team. I loved making friends doing the show. Amber is vibrant and half my age, and she hasn't got a care in the world. I could learn some stuff from her. She has a firm belief that she should be treated like a princess by men. You need only not answer one of her messages for twenty minutes and she will block your number and unfollow you on Instagram. She tells me to block them all and just start again; I tell her it's not so easy when you're in your forties!

'Watch them all come back when I delete them,' she told me that night in the car. Sure enough, there they all were, messaging her a few minutes later.

We had had such a fun night. We did that thing where one event ends and everyone decides it's a great idea to go on somewhere else for 'just one more round'.

After the second venue, I felt ready to go home, but Amber was staying at mine and wasn't ready to leave yet, and I didn't want to be the friend that puts a stop to all the fun. In the early hours, we ended up going to a lock-in at a bar in Clapham with sticky floors. As I knocked on the door, I kept my head down. I knew that was not a picture I needed in the papers! In my head, I'd decided I'd stay for one drink and then it'd be home time, but then the owner rocked up with a bottle of champagne and I felt even more obliged to stay – the people-pleaser in me was clearly still alive and kicking. By 5 a.m., I was still plotting my escape, but everyone else seemed to be going strong. I gave Amber the classic 'let's leave' eye – let's be honest, who hasn't done that one before on a night out? – but she was having the time of her life. When we finally left, it was almost morning, so someone suggested we head to Vingt Quatre, which is open twenty-four hours, to get some beans on toast and another round. It was 6.30 a.m., and there we were, eating breakfast and having a drink.

As we got out of the taxi, I even took a picture of us outside the house for posterity. It had been two decades since I had come home when the birds were singing and the sun was shining. It felt so great to not have any cares or worries. The boys hadn't been with me that night, so it'd been the perfect moment for a girls' night out.

We got up at 2 p.m. the next day to be faced with my mum's raised eyebrows – and it felt great. It was like I was finally able to do all the things I had missed out on in my twenties. I had no one to answer to, and for once my time was my own. It was not about work or my family and I didn't need to worry that my night out might affect someone else. It felt so liberating. For once, it was just about me.

Why does everyone think that life finishes once you have been through a big break-up or divorce? Your life isn't over: it's simply a new beginning. Different, yes, but certainly no less fun.

x x x

Divorce has always been painted in such a negative light, but I'm a firm believer that with change come new beginnings. It might sound clichéd, but you do always have to look for the light in life. The sad thing is that society seems set on putting divorced women in a box. I don't like to generalise, but in my experience, as a woman, you are given a different level of respect when you go through a divorce or break-up after a long relationship. Somehow, it is deemed acceptable for a man to get divorced, then date whoever they want and move on, but it doesn't seem to be the same for women. Women aren't allowed to be resilient, because it's seen as intimidating. Years after you divorce, you continue to be labelled as 'down and out', 'struggling', or 'sad'. The implication is that you're simply too emotional to ever overcome heartbreak. We've seen this story told time and time again. I'm know I'm not the first woman to have been perceived in this way, and I won't be the last either, but it's so damaging to generalise our experiences and assume that we're victims.

The worst thing is when you bump into someone you haven't seen for a while, who doesn't know you that well, and they feel sorry for you. They always use the same voice, and you can see the pity in their eyes as they say: 'How are you? I feel so sad for you. You really are having a tough time, aren't you?'

I could stand there and say, 'No, honestly, I'm doing, fine,' until the cows come home, but it never seems to register. People have a fixed idea of how a divorced woman must feel and act and they seem determined to stick to it. It's a truly harmful and unfair stereotype, and one that we need to overcome.

Divorced women are often viewed with an air of suspicion. When men move on, often with a younger partner, everyone seems to think it's fine. If I was to be pictured out with someone much older than me, I would be called a 'gold-digger'; if it was someone much younger, I would be called a 'cougar'. Either way, it is a hard line to tread, and a fight which you cannot really win.

There's an established myth of the ideal woman that we all go along with. Perhaps it's because we prefer easy narratives; perhaps, in some ways, we just expect women to fit a mould. For twenty years, I feel like I was the archetypal 'perfect' wife. I had a pop career, but gave it up for my family; I dressed appropriately and said the right things; I was married to a sportsman and had a nice life; and I never rocked the boat. All those neat little boxes were ticked, yet the first time there was a big, fat cross in a box, everything went completely off course. I had fucked up the list, and the perfect image had been shattered. Sometimes I wonder: if my public persona had been different, and if I'd been more fearless during my marriage, might the backlash when it ended have been somehow less ferocious? I'm sure there are men out there who also have a rough ride, and I know it takes them time to get back up and out there, too. But I think women also have to deal with a whole sidecar of unwanted judgement.

This is not an experience that is unique to me. I've found talking to other women who have gone through similar break-ups to be truly eye-opening. They, too, have suffered judgement from family, friends or people in their community. However the situation between a couple might appear from the outside, no one really knows what goes on behind closed doors. So it's important not to try to insert yourself into a relationship or pronounce judgements on a friend's break-up. There can be all sorts of reasons for relationships ending. I think outsiders and onlookers, however close they are to a couple, should embrace that couple's choice to separate – the most important thing is to offer support when it's needed.

There is also the issue of friendships and those grey areas around family and mutual friends. Breaking up with someone is always going to be tough, but those severed links with the people around you can also feel hard. When you're in a relationship, you embrace everything about your partner, and you form strong bonds with the people they're closest to. Recently, a friend came round who I hadn't seen for a while. I got quite upset and I told her I missed my girlfriends who I'd got to know when I was with Jamie. It's hard, because these women were my friends: we went on holiday together, went out for dinner together, and shared countless special memories. While they still enjoy their couples' nights out – birthday parties, Christmas dos, drinks and the like, I'm only invited for coffee. All of a sudden, I'm the single friend who doesn't get invited to the couples' parties.

When a couple goes through a break-up, it can become an awkward game of picking sides. Friends are put in an uncomfortable position by feeling they have to choose, and it's not fair on anyone. You can end up feeling so isolated. Having gone through my break-up, it's never been clearer to me how important it is to make sure everyone feels included. Out of all the friends Jamie and I shared, the only people who have made a point of still inviting me to their events are Jimmy Carr and his wife. They have tried to be diplomatic and made it clear that both Jamie and I would always be invited to their parties. Whether we wanted to go or felt comfortable going was entirely down to us; the invitation was there. I don't think Jimmy will ever know what that meant to me, but in those moments where I felt lost and alone, it meant the world.

Not many of my 'couples' friendships that were based around Jamie are still around. If I see them, I am polite and go through the motions, but there are not many invites these days. When you see weddings and big parties online, it can be pretty hard to swallow. I feel that everyone took their side, and in some cases this meant cutting me off completely. But in a way, maybe it's for the best. If they are the kind of people that don't want to be my friend or keep in touch, that's fine. It just shows they weren't true friends. When I speak to other women who have been through break-ups, they have reassured me that I am not the only person that this has happened to.

I am so grateful to my true friends, those who have stuck with me through thick and thin. It's OK to accept that you have different friends in your life for different reasons and at different times. There are people who come and go, and then you have the stayers: the people who stick with you.

I am someone who finds it hard to be on my own. I rely on the company of my friends, so I think friendship might be more important to me than it is to other people. I had great childhood friendships, with a good group of friends who stayed by my side throughout school and afterwards – and my friend Charli is still one of the people I am closest to today. She is zany and fun, but I know I can always count on her. At one time, there was loads written about how she was 'leading me astray' because she works as a dominatrix – but she has been one of my best friends for thirty-five years. Charli wasn't really included in my 'couples' friendships when I was married, and I am embarrassed that I let that happen. One of the great things that has come out of getting divorced has been being able to invest in friendships I may have neglected. Charli is such an important part of my life. I have learned to be proud of my friends and the individuals they are: they don't need to tick any boxes either. When the shit hits the fan, the ones that turn up in a gold catsuit are the ones who are there for you.

I am not very quick at making friends, and I can count them on one hand. I find it hard to trust people and I am bad at letting people in, but once you have earned my trust, you can't get rid of me and I am in it for the long haul. I never really had any 'showbiz' friends – the person I was always closest to was Caroline. We could talk to each other about our relationships and lives and there was never any judgement. I also knew I could trust her and I knew that whatever we told each other would stay between us.

I am also really lucky in my management now, who have become close to me on a friendship level as well as a professional one. I feel like it is more of a partnership as I've been in the music industry for so long. I respect their advice and guidance and always take it, but it feels like we are equals. I don't take ownership of a lot, but when it's something I believe in, I do. All these people have kept my head above water. Even when I have been in the depths of despair and having the worst time, my friends could always make me laugh.

The older I get, the more ruthless I become when it comes to cutting people out of my life who are toxic – you can call me 'Savage Lou'! – because I think it's pointless to maintain a friendship or a relationship if it's not working for you. I am always very invested and it takes me a while to 'let go'. We have all had those friends (or guys) who answer your text messages sometimes and not others. I don't get it. The only time I don't answer a text is if I am not interested in speaking to someone, and then I will always make it quite clear that I am not on board with the friendship or relationship. Who has time for playing games? Life can be so unsettled as it is: no one needs the 'in and outers', those people that pop up and then disappear off the radar for months. Once upon a time, I would follow up with a text message to ask that person if they were OK. Now? No way. If I have to chase,

I can't be bothered. You can only offer an olive branch and let someone know that you are there. If they don't pick up on it, then so be it. This stands for friendships, as well as relationships.

One of my great friends now is Emma, who is an intuitive hands-on healer, clairvoyant and meditation teacher. Working with her and embracing this part of my life has definitely helped me move on from my divorce and figure out what I need now in my life. Believe me when I say that I was the last person to ever be into spiritual stuff. Before meeting Emma, I had never heard much about this sort of therapy. I am also no good at deep breathing and meditation, because I am far too impatient. I prefer to get up and do the vacuuming! As I mentioned before, I have previously seen a couple of psychiatrists and counsellors because I was really struggling, but I was never honest with them or opened up about how I really felt. I was feeling very confused at the time and could not get my head around anything, so I didn't really give it a chance.

A year or so after my divorce, I did go to see Emma because mutual friends had told me she was great, but after that initial appointment, I didn't see her again for a year. I wasn't that I didn't like her or think it was good, it's just that my head wasn't in the right place at that time. During the year that followed, I became quite friendly with her sister, Becky, so I got to know Emma and we went out with friends, but we didn't talk about her work. But then, one night when I was dealing with terrible anxiety, I phoned Becky. I felt like I could not get any air in my lungs: it was like my body was shutting down. Becky put me on the phone to Emma, who talked me down. After talking to her that night, I felt much better, and I started going to see her more regularly. By trusting Emma and letting her in, I think I have really benefited. For me, developing a friendship with her enabled me to take that leap.

Emma uses a mixture of approaches, including energy healing and meditative techniques. I don't know why it works, but alongside the energy cleansing and therapies she does, she also gives amazing advice. It can be as out there as talking about things she can see happening in my future, to simply unpicking certain emotions or situations with me so that I can understand myself better. Through my sessions with her, I have learned to look inwards for answers and come up with them myself, rather than searching for validation from elsewhere. I've become more open-minded and I see it as another way to embrace life. I know people might think that I want to believe what she says because we are all looking for answers and ways to make ourselves feel better, but for me, it helps me to not question myself. It allows me to listen to myself in a slightly deeper way. I look at everything differently now, and I am grateful for the insight.

I never really had the chance to date when I was young. I went straight from being in a pop group to my solo career, then being married. I was never the girl in the club that would get asked out by different boys. When we were in Eternal, no one would dare come up to us because we were always surrounded by security guards. I did have one relationship, but then I was single until I met Jamie. I never had the time to go out and have different relationships and learn, so it was almost like I had to do that twenty years later than everyone else.

Dating as a divorced woman in your forties is really hard. I haven't done much at all since my divorce, other than going on a few dates a year or so afterwards. I think I needed to have some fun and get it out of my system. Fifty-year-old men seem to want to date thirty-year-old women, while younger men are happy to date women in their forties, but only for a few months – they seem to like the fact that you have your own life and are successful, and will not 'need' anything from them. I've realised I cannot date anyone under thirty-five (maybe thirty – I don't want to reduce my options too much!), so if you're younger than that, please do not apply. Men of my age, especially those who don't have their own family yet, generally want to meet someone to have kids with. So it is really hard to meet people.

The fact that my life comes with a lot of press attention makes things even more complicated. Whoever publicly dates me is going to have to really like me a lot, as they'll need to be able to put up with the kind of scrutiny I am often under. It is not easy – they would have to be one tough cookie. There is a dating app for people in the public eye called Raya, but I am too embarrassed to go on it. I could never date anyone else in the public eye – that would be the last thing I want. Ultimately, it just creates another barrier and makes it harder for me to let my guard down and trust them. I'd love to meet somebody who I could have an amazing time with, who is strong enough to deal with the circus and who would be happy to be with the real me.

I know that I need to 'change my brief' as my friends always tell me. Unfortunately, I think I'm often attracted to people who let me down and don't make me feel good about myself because that is what I am used to. I know that I need to learn to feel worthy of the whole shebang. When you are coming out of a relationship, it's important to look at why it has not worked, and to consider looking for something different. I also find it really hard when people tell me that my DMs must be jammed with men asking me out. The opposite is true. It would be nice to be asked out a bit more.

I did briefly use a dating app and was ghosted. I had what I thought was a good chat with a guy, and then one day he asked me what I was up to. I said, 'Oh, I'm just going for a bike ride.' And that was the end of that. It's been five months and no reply. I'm just sitting here wondering what was it that I said? Are bike rides that unattractive? But basically, this is a way to say the new world of dating is so opaque and difficult to navigate. It's easy to feel that you've done or said something wrong, when in reality it's not on you.

I know the boys would love for me to meet someone.

I was talking to Charley one day about how I'd met a guy who wanted to bring the conversation over to Snapchat, and immediately he was like, 'Mum, no.' Apparently, the only reason you want to Snapchat is if you've already got a partner or you just want to share explicit photos – who knew that I'd be getting dating advice from my son?

I'm making this new time in my life count. Now is my time and I see it as another chance to find true happiness and fulfilment in both my personal and professional lives. I have to look forward to what the future might bring. Any day now, something amazing might sweep me off my feet, whether that something is my career, my dream man, or something else entirely. I am excited about all the possibilities out there.

I love this quote by Eleanor Roosevelt: 'The future belongs to those who believe in the beauty of their dreams.'

You've Got This . . .

New starts are not always easy

Everyone copes differently, and people's individual circumstances are always unique. I don't think there is any timeline for recovering and starting again after a divorce. There will be days you feel fantastic and are glad it is over, and other days when the opposite is true. I think this is completely normal.

Women put a lot of pressure on themselves to instantly 'move on', but it is normal to grieve the end of any relationship. Give yourself space to feel however you are feeling. Time is a healer, but from personal experience, it can be elastic, so ...

How can you thrive after a break-up or divorce?

So many people go through big relationship break-ups. It may feel like the worst thing in the world when you are going through it, but it means you can move forwards with your life. A divorce or a break-up does not mean that your life is over: it's a new start and it can be a huge catalyst for change. You have no choice but to move on, and you can mould your future in a way that makes you feel happier and more fulfilled.

Other people's judgement and lack of respect for me are still one of the hardest things to deal with

Dealing with judgement from others when I am struggling, sad and lonely, is pretty tedious. I don't need other people's judgement – or pity. I am fine, thank you! Sadly, the judgement will always be there. Whether a woman is getting a divorce at twenty-five or forty, people still think and do the same things and have similar reactions. This is a societal problem and it's one women have to tackle. If we break out of the narrative of being the perfect wife and mother and get divorced, it's like we don't 'fit' anywhere any more and it makes people feel uncomfortable. This is ridiculous. People need to be more open-minded and understand that there can be many reasons for any divorce. There will always be stuff that has happened or gone down, but it doesn't mean people have to talk openly about what is behind their decision. No one ever knows what really happens in a relationship. The answer? Respect someone's decision to walk away. If you are the person breaking up with your partner, know that there is nothing wrong with you. Very few relationships meet our childhood expectations of 'happily ever after' – it doesn't mean you have failed, or that you will never find happiness yourself.

What do smart women do after a break-up?

One of the most important things is to lean on your friends. I have always been very lucky in having so many wonderful friends, but going through my break-up really showed me just how valuable my true friends are. I treasure my friendships so much because I love being surrounded by people, so suddenly being single after twenty years meant I needed them more than ever.

My friendships have changed over the years, but true friends will never judge you or make you feel guilty for mistakes you make. Good friendships are empowering, motivating, and a source of comfort and encouragement. My friends can pick me up and make me laugh, even when I am on the floor. The people who pick up the pieces, check in every day, and genuinely care, are the friends I am most grateful for.

Over the years, I have learned the value of professional friendships that develop through work, and how these partnerships can also become a really valuable part of moving forwards. They sit outside of the rest of your life and they celebrate your professional successes because they are part of it. Having those different layers of friendship is really important.

I read this quote by Oprah Winfrey recently, and it really rang true: 'Everyone wants to ride with you in the limo, but what you want is someone who will take the bus with you when the limo breaks down.'

Don't be afraid to ask for help

It took me a while to find the right sort of therapy for me, but I am grateful that I have learned to explore my spiritual side. I think therapy is important when you need an outlet in life that goes beyond talking to friends, who may perhaps know your life too well. Without talking to someone neutral, it can be hard to come up with the right answers. For some people, more practical guidance might be important, but for me, spirituality has allowed me to look at my complicated emotions and responses more closely, to feel OK about feeling things more deeply, and to listen to my own needs. I have become more open to different ideas around spirituality generally. Just the other night, I had a group of girlfriends over and we planted prayer sticks in the garden. We wrote down our hopes and wishes on the sticks before burying them, and it was incredibly therapeutic. Perhaps nothing will come of the prayer sticks, but it was another opportunity to really focus on me and what I want, and a good way to get the girls together for some wine – what's not to like? You can make spirituality work for you. It's really about finding a way to focus on yourself, have fun and look to the future.

Take the opportunity to make new traditions

Some of the hardest times after any break-up or loss are Christmases, birthdays, or other holidays, but it is important not to let your life stand still: find other ways to celebrate that are special. You can ditch any old traditions that no longer suit you, go crazy or scale back, and assemble a new crew of people to have fun with. Sometimes it is little things that can make the biggest difference. I find laughter the simplest way to switch my mood.

The big one . . . dating after divorce

I can only be honest and say that, when it comes to dating, I am still trying to work it out. The mechanics of where to look and how to go about it are a bit of a minefield, so can I keep you posted on that front? The experts say that dating after divorce can make you rethink everything you know, and for me, this has been a good opportunity to learn to understand what I need and deserve. Breaking away from old habits and routines can be hard, but it's something I need to do for myself. As my friends say, I need to 'change my brief' and choose someone who makes me feel great and loved. Also, who you fancy and who makes your heart feel whole can be two very different things and both qualities are important. I know I deserve nothing less. I'm looking forward to meeting someone and starting again.

A second chapter – or chance – can come in many forms

Big life changes can happen for lots of reasons. I know many people go through awful stuff, far worse than what I have experienced – I am under no illusions about that. There are people who have lost family and friends they love, or have suffered terribly with their health. Sometimes changes are about different things, like taking a job in a foreign city, having kids, or deciding you don't feel that fulfilled in your current life and need to take action. My world was rocked by my divorce, but I hope that if your situation is different and you are reading this, there is stuff you can take away for yourself. Change is always difficult and can feel overwhelming. There are times in life when we might think that we are merely surviving, and that the daily rollercoaster of emotions is too much to handle. That rollercoaster might not be easy or fun, but whatever big life changes happen to you, you will get through it.

What makes you happy?

Life is busy, and I've talked a lot in this book about the way that women are often so occupied with taking care of others that they lose sight of what makes them tick. Now is the time to discover what you love to do and what makes you happy.

Don't feel exposed because one role has been stripped away. Instead, enjoy rediscovering what makes you *you*. I don't have any room for negativity any more, and I have learned that I need to fill my life with positivity and good people.

Conclusion

YOU *ARE* ALWAYS
GOOD ENOUGH

*W*hat does it mean to thrive and find true happiness? I have at least got some stuff worked out, and I hope that some of the stories and ideas that I've shared in this book will be useful to you in some shape or form, regardless of your personal situation. If you are reading this and are on some kind of journey (I know, I hate that word, but that is what it is for me) know that you can't stop in your tracks and let yourself be beaten. I have learned to be true to myself and what I have achieved, without letting vicious and untrue headlines and comments deter me. Know that it is OK to have ambition and desire, whatever age you are.

I have also learned to accept the bad days. We can't always sail through life with ease, but don't let a bad day today stop you from having a good day tomorrow. Take time to trust, to listen to your heart, to do what pleases you. Ask yourself what you want from your future and what is stopping you from getting there. Have enough courage to trust yourself and be fearless. No matter what happens, you'll figure out a way to make it work. You *are* always good enough.

Always believe that the best is yet to come. Remember: you've got this.

Love, Lou x

ACKNOWLEDGEMENTS

First off, I would love to say a huge thanks to Georgina Rodgers, who helped bring *You've Got This* to life. I'd also like to thank Massive Management's Wayne, Pippa and Billy, who have had to read through this book hundreds of times; David Lazenby, from Vivienne Clore, who enabled this book to happen; Lewis, who must be so fed up of hearing all my stories; and Charli – for always telling me how it is, even when I don't want to hear it. To Simon Jones – thanks for always being there, and sorry in advance for taking up your time when this is published!

Thanks to my mum for giving me the courage to be as honest as I could whilst writing this book and of course, my boys, Chaz and Beau, for always keeping my feet firmly on the ground – I hope this book can make you proud and teach you that you should never be ashamed of how you feel.

Thanks to Little, Brown for guiding me through this process – you've been a pleasure to work with. And to everybody who has featured in my book, you've all impacted my life in a huge way – thank you for helping me to have stories to tell. I'd also like to say a huge thank-you to everyone who worked on the cover shoot: photography – Paul Farrell, hair – Bjorn Krischker, make-up – Caroline Barnes, styling – Lorna McGee.